The Open University

Social sciences: a third level course People and organizations 2 (Units 3-6)

Structure and system: basic concepts and theories

prepared by the course team

The Open University Press

People and organizations course team

Kenneth Thompson (Chairman), Senior Lecturer in Sociology, Open University.

Martin Albrow, Senior Lecturer in Sociology, University College, Cardiff.

John Beishon, Professor of Systems, Open University.

Hedy Brown, Lecturer in Social Psychology, Open University.

David Elliott, Lecturer in Engineering Science, Open University.

David Hickson, Professor of Behavioural Studies, University of Bradford.

Jill Jones, Research Officer, Goldsmiths' College, London.

Arthur McCullough, Chairman of the Organizational Analysis Research Unit, University of Bradford.

Charles McMillan, Research Fellow in Organizational Analysis, University of Bradford.

Ken Patton, Production Director, BBC.

Charles Perrow, Professor of Sociology, State University of New York, Stoney Brook.

Graeme Salaman, Lecturer in Sociology, Open University.

David Silverman, Senior Lecturer in Sociology, Goldsmiths' College, London.

Mary-Anne Speakman, Course Assistant in Sociology, Open University.

Eric Wade, Staff Tutor Social Sciences, Open University.

David Weeks, Lecturer in Sociology, City of London Polytechnic.

The Open University Press
Walton Hall, Milton Keynes
MK7 6AA

First published 1974. Reprinted 1975

Designed by the Media Development Group of the Open University.

Printed in Great Britain by
COES THE PRINTERS LIMITED
RUSTINGTON SUSSEX

ISBN 0 335 01565 4

This text forms part of an Open University course. The complete list of units in the course appears at the end of this text.

For general availability of supporting material referred to in this text, please write to the Director of Marketing, The Open University, P.O. Box 81, Walton Hall, Milton Keynes, MK7 6AT.

Further information on Open University courses may be obtained from the Admissions Office, The Open University, P.O. Box 48, Walton Hall, Milton Keynes, MK7 6AB.

Contents

Front cover: *A Nous La Liberté*, Distributed in the UK and Eire by
Connoisseur Films Ltd., 167, Oxford Street, London, W.1.

Structure and system: basic concepts and theories

Introduction to Block 2

The previous two units considered organizations in terms of their wider social and political relevances and attempted to relate the analysis of organizations both to practical political issues and events and to theoretical themes and debates initially introduced by the classical, early sociologists. Such topics obviously serve as a sensible and topical introduction to the course by displaying the overall course rationale and relating the investigation of organizations to sociological theory and social issues. This block continues this strategy with reference to the internal features of organizations.

If organizations are important it is important to understand how they operate. This is the issue addressed by these units. However, as you by now appreciate, sociology cannot and does not simply present descriptions of 'how things work', because such descriptions and accounts depend upon the choice of topic, the theoretical approach, the methodology and so on. Consequently, the units in this course will not only address the question: how do organizations work?, they will also, and at the same time, be considering: what are the assumptions lying behind this sort of account of how organizations work? What does it take for a description or analysis of an organization to be sensible?

Nowhere will this feature of the course be more apparent than in the presentation of, and reaction to, what is known as the systems approach to organizations. This approach is presented in Unit 6, and is critically considered elsewhere, particularly in David Silverman's book *The Theory of Organizations*, relevant sections of which are set reading for this block. Units 4 and 5 also contain discussions that are severely damaging to assumptions that are usually considered to be central to the systems approach. However the job of considering the advantages and disadvantages of this approach is, finally, left with the student: it is the student's responsibility to sift the various arguments and counter-arguments, revisions and modifications, and to arrive at some sort of conclusion about the weaknesses and uses of this approach to the study of organizations.

This course takes as its theme the issue of organizational control. Control means that members of the organization have their actions (and, possibly, attitudes and orientations) determined, or influenced by membership of the organization. This process involves power. It would be impossible to consider organizational control without considering the nature of power within organizations, how it is distributed, how it originates. Such issues constitute the topics of Unit 3. Two points of particular importance are made by this unit. First, that despite the crucial importance of organizational power in any attempt to study organizations, the concept suffers from a wealth of overlapping and conflicting definitions and applications. Therefore conceptual and theoretical debate is essential to any serious interest in organizations, or anything else. This point is made frequently in these units. Secondly, David Hickson and Arthur McCullough point out the connection between power and uncertainty, a point that is developed by Hickson *et al.* in Salaman and Thompson (1973). Senior members of organizations will attempt to reduce uncertainty about the behaviour of subordinates by limiting and controlling their activities. For this they need power. At the same time members of the organization will attempt to create or negotiate some area of discretion, of creativity, and consequently also, of uncertainty. And capacity to cope with organizational uncertainty is a source of power.

The fact that organizations involve attempts to reduce uncertainty, and to create order and stability (indeed this stability is usually what is meant by an organization) is the central topic of Units 4 and 5, which have been written together and follow one another without a break. These units consider the concept organizational structure and the ways in which organizations are structured, or display structure. This concept is used to refer to the most dramatic and obvious feature of organizations: the way they involve a relatively stable patterning of activities over time. And the two units consider the origins of this structure and its relationship to various factors that have been considered as determinants of organizational structure. These units also discuss a number of classifications of organization in terms of the suggested relationships between features of organizations, and other factors. Although noting the importance of the concept structure with respect to organizations these units also stress the variable, but existent possibility of choice that lies behind the attempts to impose structure on organizations, and the behaviours which give rise to the emergent regularity that is considered as organizational structure. Finally, these units devote attention to the variety of forms of control employed by organizations, since there is reason to believe, and many studies support the idea, that organizations make use of more than one method of controlling personnel.

The systems unit has already been mentioned. The systems approach to organizations, outlined in Unit 6, is particularly interesting – and problematic – because it derives from a model of functional interdependence – systems theory – which comes from outside sociological theorizing and which, its enthusiasts claim, is applicable to many sorts of phenomena, and many academic disciplines. Here, possibly, lie its main advantages and deficiencies. In particular it will be claimed that with respect to the sociological study of organizations, systems theory suffers from a commitment to an excessively abstract level of generalization, and, usually, from a relative lack of interest in, or concern about, developments and debates within sociological theory and research which are critical of the application of systems theory to social phenomena. In Unit 6 an expert on systems theory, from the Technology Faculty of the Open University, presents the main features and concepts of this approach. On the whole he has left the work of criticism and evaluation to other writers (Silverman, Buckley) and, finally, to the student.

Unit 3 Power in organizations
David J. Hickson
Arthur E. McCullough

Section cover: *Kes*, released through United Artists

Contents Unit 3

Reading for this unit

The following minimum reading should be done either prior to studying this unit or in conjunction with it, at the points indicated in the unit. (For full references see References at the end of the unit.)

1 Peter M. Blau and Richard A. Schoenherr 'New Forms of Power' in Graeme Salaman and Kenneth Thompson (eds) *People and Organizations* (the Reader) pp. 13–24. (This was part of the set reading for Unit 1 and so it need only be looked at sufficiently to refresh your memory.)

2 Derek S. Pugh and David J. Hickson, 'The Comparative Study of Organizations' in Salaman and Thompson (eds) pp. 50–66.

3 John Child, 'Organizational Structure, Environment and Performance: The Role of Strategic Choice in Salaman and Thompson (eds) pp. 91–107.

4 David J. Hickson *et al.* 'A Strategic Contingencies Theory of Intraorganizational Power' in Salaman and Thompson (eds) pp. 174–89.

5 Fred E. Katz, 'Integrative and Adaptive Uses of Autonomy: Worker Autonomy in Factories' in Salaman and Thompson (eds) pp. 190–204.

6 Amitai Etzioni, 'Compliance Theory' in Oscar Grusky and George A. Miller (eds) *The Sociology of Organizations* (set book) pp. 103–26.

7 There are useful sections in David Dunkerley, *The Study of Organizations*, which was recommended as preparatory reading for this course. If you have access to a copy you should look again at the section on Michels in chapter 1, Weber in chapter 2, and chapters 3 and 4 (especially the sections on Blau and Scott, and Etzioni).

8 If you have time it is worth looking at R. Michels, 'Oligarchy' in Grusky and Miller (eds) pp. 25–43.

Power in organizations

Aims and objectives

The aim of this unit can be stated simply: first to describe power in organizations, and then to begin to analyse it. The unit is in seven sections:

1 The concept of power: a brief look at terminology, and a working definition of power.
2 Hierarchical power: how power is distributed 'up and down' organizations.
3 The power of sub-units: how power is distributed 'across' organizations, paying most attention to departmental power.
4 Power and decision making: how power shapes decision processes and premises.
5 Resources: some analyses of the kinds of resources used for power in organizations.
6 Responses (or 'effects'): some analyses of the response of those affected by the use of resources for power.
7 Some problems and variables: the difficulties of 'invisible power'; some major variables implicit in the concepts underlying the whole topic.

1 The concept of power

1.1 Definition

Any understanding of organizations must take account of the differential distribution of power between positions in them, and between the occupants of those positions. At its most obvious, doctors have more power than nurses, and some doctors have more power than others: managers have more power than clerks, and some managers have more power than others: some factories are said to be 'sales dominated' and some 'production dominated'. Power is the essence of organization, from Weber's analysis of its legitimation (Dunkerley 1972 p. 17; and Unit 1), which underlies the structure of an organization, to the often unnoticed control inherent in social interaction within an organization (Units 7, 8 and 9).

Power is the essence of organization

The study of power is plagued by terminological confusion. Words abound such as authority, influence, coercion, force, domination, and control. Each author's definition of such terms has to be checked to see what is meant, and even then the definitions are not always clear. Here we shall use the word power as the generic term to encompass all the subtleties.

Most theorists are agreed, first, that power means *affecting others*, though some stress its effects as a subtle moulding of ways of thought, some stress power as limiting others' freedom of choice among alternatives, and some stress its direct impact in changing behaviour. Second, if power affects others, then it is by the availability of *resources*, for example wealth, or status of a kind which allows the giving of instructions to subordinates, or expert knowledge which overrides other suggestions. Third, whoever has access to these resources must be in a position – have the *capacity* – to take advantage of them. So, for our purposes in examining power in work organizations we can regard *power as the capacity to use resources to affect others*.

Definition of power

So we are not concerned with autonomy, which we will regard as an organization member's control of his own behaviour, as distinct from his power over the behaviour of others.

The problems of defining power have been discussed by many authors, including Bierstadt (1950), Dahl (1968), and Cartwright (1965). Difficulties such as whether power occurs only if its effects are deliberately intended and/or resisted and whether power may be potential or latent in the sense that others anticipate the use of power and act accordingly, are exposed by writers such as March (1955, 1957), Emerson (1962),

Wrong (1968), and Bachrach and Baratz (1962). These and other authors listed by Hickson *et al.* (1973) can be referred to for an examination of such problems which will not be discussed here.

However, it is useful to know three variables of power which Kaplan (1964 pp. 14 and 15) has defined clearly. These are:

Three variables – weight, domain and scope

Weight (or amount of effect on others): i.e. how far 'A can at his choice affect the probability that B will act in a certain way in certain circumstances'.

Domain: i.e. 'the range of persons or groups influenced'.

Scope: i.e. 'the range of . . . responses whose probabilities are affected'.

For example, the power of a workers' leader in a factory may have such *weight* that at a word from him his fellow workers down tools without question, or so little weight that it takes him weeks of persuasion to get a response. His *domain* may be every worker in the plant all of whom strike, or only his immediate workmates. Although the *scope* of his power includes behaviour on the job it may stop short of determining the political party allegiances of those who accept his power over their work.

In Sections 2, 3 and 4 we will now examine how power is distributed within organizations, and then in the subsequent sections analyse the resources on which power is based and look at some sorts of explanations of these distributions of power that have been put forward.

SAQ 1 Can there be organization without power?

2 Hierarchical power

2.1 Official hierarchy

The two structural fundamentals of organization, hierarchy and division of labour, are each inevitably bound up with power in organizations. We will look at power first from the perspective of hierarchy, and then from the perspective of the division of labour as that is represented by sub-units (or departments or sections).

Hierarchy and division of labour in relation to power

The two concepts overlap, since hierarchy is partly a division of labour because the supervisory and administrative tasks of bosses differ from the tasks of those who are their subordinates: but primarily, hierarchy is a division of power. The higher the level in the hierarchy, the greater the recognized right – the authority – to control the use of resources and the behaviour of others. For instance, managers may allocate money, and so be able to buy machinery, or alter wages and thereby attempt to affect the behaviour of personnel below them in the hierarchy: workers usually can do neither.

Figure 1 shows a conventional organization chart of a factory. Conventional, that is, except for the written characters on it which very few readers of this unit will be able to comprehend. The chart comes from a Japanese factory. Yet it is immediately recognized for what it is, irrespective of the language of its written content: the formal hierarchy of authority is plain to see. It proceeds level by level from a single top position whose authority is greater than that of any other single position (which is not to say that its authority is absolute, greater than that of any combination of others in the organization).

The chart shows the overwhelmingly prevalent type of hierarchy, but there are other variations, mainly multiple apexes. For example, a group of medical practitioners may come together in a small health centre but avoid naming any one as having the final say: hospitals often have three sub-hierarchies, of doctors, of nurses, and of administrative and ancillary personnel, without it being clear whether the senior medical consultant, the matron, or the hospital secretary or executive, is at the top: in a trade union, the part-time president and the full-time secretary may jostle for position: some companies claim to be run by a committee with a non-executive chairman. But these are the exceptions.

Figure 1 **Japanese organization chart** Source: The Matsushita Electronics Corporation Visitors Guide

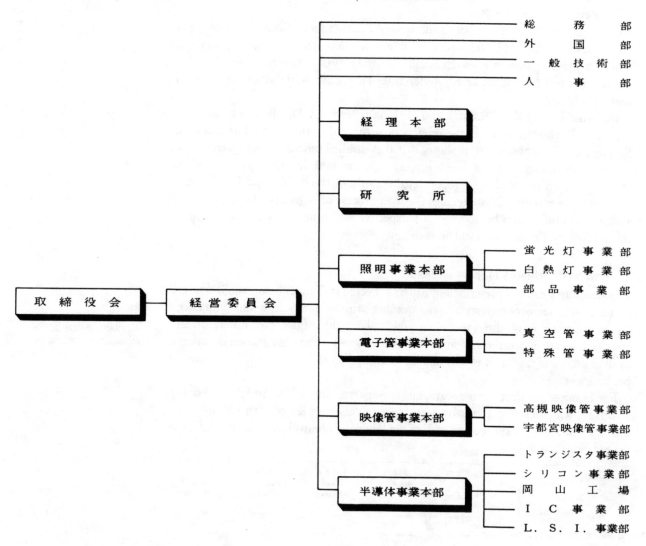

2.2 Hierarchical power distribution

Pugh and Hickson, in their article, 'The Comparative Study of Organizations' (Salaman and Thompson 1973 pp. 50–66) present a chart of the characteristics of six heterogeneous British organizations: a municipal (local government) department, assorted private companies, state-owned manufacturing, and a retailing chain. The key indicates that the fifth bar of each organization's histogram represents its comparative degree of centralization of formal decision making authority. You can see that the centralization of the two governmental or publicly owned organizations is comparatively high. Why should this be? Pugh and Hickson suggest that demands for decisions to be made openly, in public scrutiny, are a pressure for decisions to be referred upwards to representative committees and councils (so that the public who demand democratic control will also fume at the 'bureaucratic' delay thereby created?!). But they also suggest that a similar pressure for accountability in the use of resources forces the small units of large *private* combines to refer decisions upwards.

Centralization and accountability

In contrast, organizations C and D in the same figure show comparatively high Functional specialization, Formalization, and Standardization, which in combination amount to highly bureaucratic administration – or, as Pugh and Hickson call it, 'structuring of activities' of employees. That is, control is maintained not so much by centralizing decisions towards the top but by setting prescribed tasks, rules, and procedures to regulate behaviour (see Units 5, 8 and 9). It is a less visible form of power, which sets the limits of what others may do, shapes the premises by which

Decentralization and specification

they decide, and then delegates authority within these constraints; a kind of freedom of manoeuvre within bounds.

So subordinates can either await the bosses' decision (centralization) or use their own discretion within the rules they have learned (decentralization). In either case power is present, though research results imply that most people prefer the latter where they feel free of irksome interference. They have some autonomy, even if they have little power.

But what kind of data are Pugh and Hickson reporting? (Details can be found in papers by Pugh *et al.* listed in the references at the end of this unit.) The extract in Salaman and Thompson (1973) shows that they studied official authority levels, i.e. the levels in the hierarchy at which top management said decisions were taken and acted upon (Whisler *et al.* 1967, report an alternative method of doing this). Yet more goes into power than this: it includes the total process of influence of one person by another, and one group by another. A perspective which may pick up something of this is taken by Tannenbaum and his colleagues.

2.3 How hierarchy looks to those involved

Tannenbaum's method (described in papers collected in Tannenbaum 1968) is to ask organization members to respond on a questionnaire to questions about 'influence'. There are many possibilities including asking about the influence of different hierarchical levels (e.g. managers or supervisors or workers) in the organization in general, or over each other, or as it ideally should be compared to how it actually appears to be, and so on.

Members' perception of influence possessed by different levels in hierarchy

For example, in thirty-two geographically separate sites of an American delivery company, which carried goods by road, respondents were asked: 'In general, how much say or influence do you feel each of the following groups has on what goes on in your station?', as follows:

	Little or no influence	Some influence	Quite a bit of influence	A great deal of influence	A very great deal of influence
Your station manager	——	——	——	——	——
The other supervisors in your station	——	——	——	——	——
The men in your station	——	——	——	——	——

The same question was repeated on what the influence of each 'should' be. Figure 2 shows the result (full details are on pp. 73–9 in Tannenbaum 1968). It plots the average scores of the responses of supervisors and of non-supervisors (men). Each respondent can score from 1.0, little influence, to 5.0, a very great deal, on his view of each of the three hierarchical levels.

Both supervisors and men see influence as roughly following an orderly step by step hierarchical sequence, but the men think they themselves *should* have more influence than they feel they do have. That is, the hierarchy of power should not be so 'steep', and the slope of the control graph, as it is called, should not be so negative in direction.

As in this example, personnel in industrial or business organizations usually perceive these as more hierarchical in power terms than organizations with some 'voluntary' (non-paid) membership appear to be to their members. In these latter organizations, such as trade unions, or the local branches of the American League of Women Voters, which were once studied, the slope of the control graph is not so steeply negative or, indeed, may be positive. That is, in some American Unions the members were seen as having as much or more influence than the officials who headed the hierarchy. The literature about organizations which employ substantial proportions of highly trained professional personnel, such as universities and research institutes, suggests that these, too, have a less hierarchical power distribution than is common in

Figure 2 Average control curves for 32 stations of a delivery company: Actual and ideal control – non-supervisors and supervisors Source: Tannenbaum, *Control in Organization* (p.78). Copyright © 1968 by McGraw-Hill. Used with permission of McGraw-Hill Book Company.

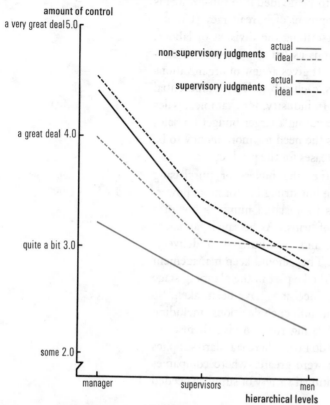

industry and commerce (professional training is an alternative control, as we will see in Units 4 and 5).

Whatever the pressures, whatever the spread of decisions (in Pugh and Hickson's terms) or the slope of the graph (in Tannenbaum's terms), the balance of power rarely if ever tilts wholly one way. Few organizations have overwhelming power weight over every aspect of the behaviour of every one of their members (total scope and domain). That is, few approach what Goffman (1968) has called the 'total institution', controlling its members day and night, waking and sleeping, throughout the twenty-four hours. At times the armed forces, or religious organizations such as monasteries or nunneries, or boarding schools, or merchant ships, come close to it. Control 'off the job' is quite common, e.g. senior civil servants in Britain are not allowed to be active in politics. But mostly there is a deal of scope for behaviour outside such control, even 'on the job'. For example, the importing of working-class culture into the factory, with a whole range of behaviour officially unrecognized or forbidden by management, is vividly and often amusingly described by Katz and Roy in Salaman and Thompson (1973 pp. 190–204 and pp. 205–22).

Also, there is frequently delegation and participation of the kinds described by Strauss (1963) and advocated by writers such as Likert (1961), though how far this should be called 'power-equalization', as Strauss terms it, is a moot point. Welcome though it may be to the subordinates concerned to have more say in what they themselves do or in changes which may affect them, the power hierarchy continues and eventually the decision is probably taken above them.

3 The power of sub-units

3.1 Interdepartmental systems

Although organizations are bound together by a controlling hierarchy, they are at the same time shifting coalitions of interested parties. They are more or less open systems

SAQ 2 What is hierarchy?

SAQ 3a What is the main difference between the Pugh and Hickson method and Tannenbaum's method?

SAQ 3b What is left out by the methods of Pugh and Hickson and of Tannenbaum?

reconciling the multiple goals (see Units 5 and 6) of employees or managers or owners or customers or suppliers, etc. The larger an organization becomes, the more the problems in which these parties are interested tend to be divided into sub-problems and assigned to sub-units. This is part of the development of bureaucracy (Units 1 and 5, and also Unit 13), and is another way of describing the division of labour. Parsons' analysis reviewed in Unit 6 sees organizations as being composed of sub-systems designed to deal with basic system problems. It gives a view of organizations as being inter-sub-unit or inter-departmental systems, each sub-unit with differential power, each pursuing its own ends within the whole. In industry, for example, a sales department may see its marketing campaign as necessitating a larger budget for sales staff salaries and expenses, whilst production stresses the need for more money to be invested in stocks of raw materials in case demand increases for the product.

Strauss (1962) found that 'purchasing agents' (i.e. the buyers or purchasing managers in firms he studied) were in a weak position, but struggling for more power. (He observed, interviewed, and gave questionnaires to unstated numbers out of a total of 142 purchasing agents studied in a number of firms.) As he saw it, an agent has two primary tasks, placing orders for supplies, and expediting their delivery. But agents feel they should do much more than this. They should keep management informed on new materials, on prices, etc., and should take part in the planning stage of new products, not merely place orders after all the decisions have been taken. So the agents studied used a variety of tactics to try and influence decisions, including exploiting friends in other departments, and manipulating rules to give themselves greater power to affect what happened. Agents could do little where standard supplies were routinely bought, but their chances of power were greater where companies made goods to customer order so that there was a continual variety of supplies needed for varying products.

Any change, of course, may favour some sub-unit(s) rather than others. New machinery, for example, which runs with very little maintenance required, may help a production department, but put the maintenance engineers in a precarious position. When Normann (1971) followed the development of new products in twelve Swedish companies in food processing, packaging, pharmaceuticals, construction, electronics, and engineering, he found that the departmental power structure served as a filter for new ideas. Departments attempted to mould changes to their own viewpoint. This is corroborated by Carter (1971 p. 418) who traced major decisions in an American computer company, and reports that when a decision was to be made, 'By bargaining within departments the staff would preprocess investments to ensure that projects submitted for the president's consideration fitted the wishes of the members of the department.' (Carter 1971 p. 418.)

3.2 Generalization

It is clear that the pattern of power among sub-units differs from one organization to the next, but research has not yet established whether there is sufficient stability and uniformity to enable wide descriptive generalizations.

In the United States, Zald (1962) has inferred that as the aims of penal institutions shift from punishment to treatment, so power slips away from the 'custodial' staff. Clark (1956) has analysed educational institutions. But most of the meagre research has been in industrial organizations.

For instance, Hinings et al. (1973) tested the power theory put forward by Hickson et al. (1973 pp. 174–89) in five breweries and two cardboard container factories in Canada and the United States. They found that production was consistently more powerful than marketing, engineering, or accounting. In each organization these were the only four sub-units, making a complete interdepartmental system. A range of power data were obtained from detailed interviewing about departmental activities,

Pursuit of departmental goals and power

Most research done on industrial organizations

Production departments most powerful

Table 1 Perceived power (weight) of 4 sub-units in organization S (brewery)
On each of 17 issues, means of the questionnaire ratings of every sub-unit by heads of all 4 sub-units (scores at or above the mean for the Table underlined)

17 ISSUES, as allocated to task areas (or functions)

SUB-UNITS	Sales area					Engineering area		Production area				Finance area			Personnel area (salary training)			Overall means
	marketing strategies	introduction of new products	product packaging	price	interpretation of liquor regulations	obtaining equipment	operating performance of equipment	obtaining raw materials	product quality	production efficiency	overall production plan	overall capital budget	overall non-capital budget	reviews of the non-capital budget	salary revision	personnel training and development	personnel and labor relations	
Accounting	1.5	1.5	1.5	4.5	2.75	2.75	1.75	2.0	1.0	2.25	2.75	4.0	3.75	3.5	3.25	3.5	3.25	2.7
Engineering	1.25	1.75	3.25	1.0	1.5	4.25	5.0	2.25	2.75	4.75	2.5	3.5	2.75	2.5	1.75	2.75	1.5	2.7
Marketing	5.0	5.0	3.5	3.0	4.5	1.75	2.0	2.0	2.75	2.0	2.25	2.75	2.75	2.5	2.25	3.0	2.25	2.9
Production	3.25	3.75	4.0	2.0	2.5	4.5	4.5	5.0	5.0	5.0	4.0	3.5	2.75	2.5	2.25	3.25	3.0	3.6

Source: Hinings *et al.* 1973 to appear.

from questionnaires, and from chief executives' definitions of departmental authority. All data presented a consistent picture over multiple analyses. An example from questionnaire data alone is given in Table 1. In this small branch brewery of 300 employees, the heads of all four departments or sub-units were asked to rate their own and each of the other departments on five point scales, from have 'very great influence' to 'little influence', on each of the seventeen issues listed in the Table. These issues were reported by the department heads to be recurrent interdepartmental topics.

Highest influence scores are underlined in the Table, picking out production not only as unchallenged within its own task area but as frequently having considerable power in the other departments' areas of work. Marketing, on the other hand, whilst dominating its own area of sales, shares that power with production and has a lesser place outside the sales area.

These results, on an unusually full range of power data but on a small sample, do not fit Perrow's (1970) picture of the dominant power of *sales* departments in the American market economy. In the small units Hinings *et al.* studied, the belief (in brewing) that brewing beer is a special skill, the complexities (in container production) of making a variety of special packagings, and in both brewing and container manufacture the central position of production in the organization's workflow and its involvement in everything that happens, all helped make the *production* department the most powerful. Thus far, generalizations can only be speculation.

Indeed, the maintenance or engineering section can also exert a great deal of power. In twenty-three small tobacco plants in France investigated by Crozier (1964), the maintenance personnel were able to monopolize the know-how necessary to repair machine breakdowns. Since all else ran smoothly, mostly under central administrative control from Paris head office, machine breakdowns were the only critical problem. Since the maintenance personnel could deal with the problem, they were powerful.

In studies such as these the power differences can be held to arise somehow from a department being 'critical' to an organization (to use Perrow's 1970 word). Thus Landsberger (1961) argued from the histories of three engineering firms that when

SAQ 4 Which sub-unit(s) has least power in Table 1?

Contrast with Perrow's finding

Power of maintenance department

Departmental power related to critical or strategic position

money is scarce, accounting is more powerful; when raw materials are short, purchasing is more powerful; and, conversely, when demand is insatiable, sales are less powerful.

SAQ 5 How does one sub-unit become more powerful than the rest? Can you find clues in the text?

4 Power and decision making

4.1 Decision processes

For a summary of the view of organizations as decision making systems developed by Cyert and March (1963), see Unit 12 (also, Dunkerley 1972 p. 48). Here we will briefly look at the power aspect of decision making.

Often there is a tendency to speak as if decisions are made at a single moment of time, as if they all emanated from the mythical men of decision created by the wilder Westerns and the less novel novelists. Yet even if a decision does seem to be made quickly on the spur of the moment, it is necessarily the culmination of experience which includes being influenced by others (see Unit 12). And in a crisis, though one man or a few may have to make up their minds with no chance to contact others, yet they will implicitly or explicitly weigh up the likely views of any especially powerful others.

Decisions are cumulative

Attempts to trace what leads up to a decision reveal confused sequences which suggest that the very term 'a decision' is misleading. More accurately, there are processes of decision, or many sub-decisions. The record by Cyert *et al.* (1956) of an American company's decision to install electronic data processing equipment spans no less than three years (and even then, where is its beginning and its end?), and shows that a variety of managerial and other personnel from accounting and sales departments were involved, a range of executives on a management committee, the company president, various computer company representatives and consultants, and influential outsiders met at conferences. Pettigrew's (1972) study of a similar decision in a British company shows the power of a manager who was the nexus of a similarly wide range of internal and external contacts over about five years. In short there is a maze of talking and more talking, considering and further considering, informing and re-informing, in most decision processes, excepting perhaps the more programmed, autonomous, and trivial. So decision processes are power processes.

As Lindblom (1959) points out in a provoking analysis, the optimum decision made in a detached way by exact calculation from all relevant information, somehow uncontaminated by other affairs of the world, probably does not and never did exist outside books of maths exercises. Much more likely, a process of decision making moves spasmodically within a restricted set of possibilities, priorities switching from one time to another and different aspects being weighed in the balance from one point to the next. (Simon 1947; Cyert and March 1963.) It arrives at a compromise that will do for the time being, within the bounds of power and practicability.

Table 1 lists as many as seventeen decision issues which even in rather small stable organizations (brewing plants) were recurrent and involved different departments. The most widely powerful sub-unit is Production (beer-brewing). However, whilst Production might well have the lion's share of any decision over 'obtaining raw materials' (from hops to bottle tops), as it scored much the highest influence on this issue, if it tried to alter 'product packaging' it might enter a drawn out process of reconciling the interests of the Marketing and Engineering (Maintenance) departments which are more influential on that particular issue. We have mentioned earlier the studies by Normann (1971) and Carter (1971) who found powerful departments bargaining one with another, and putting up to higher management only those innovations which fitted in with what they wanted. So some alternatives are thought of as realistic and some are ruled out, some consequences are seen and others are ignored, partly at least because of group pressures. Those interested may have power to shape the premises from which decisions ensue, and the limits of what is considered: they may shape the structure within which the decision is arrived at.

A decision, then, is arrived at within a power structure in which various interests prefer certain outcomes before even the decision process could be said to have begun. Cohen *et al.* (1972) see an organization as a collection of decision makers looking for opportunities, solutions looking for problems to which they might be the answer and feelings looking for issues on which they can be aired. It is a situation they have colourfully dubbed a 'garbage can'. To quote them:

> To understand processes within organizations, one can view a choice opportunity as a garbage can into which various kinds of problems and solutions are dumped by participants as they are generated. The mix of garbage in a single can depends on the mix of garbage available, on the labels attached to the alternative cans, on what garbage is currently being produced, and on the speed with which garbage is collected and removed from the scene. (Cohen *et al.* 1972 p. 2.)

A startling description, but not an inappropriate one.

5 Resources
5.1 Terminology
Having examined the distribution of power hierarchically, and from the perspective of sub-units, with a brief look at decisions as outcomes of power processes, we can now return to our initial definition of power. This regarded power as the capacity to use *resources* to affect others.

The notion of resources, which when used for power are usually referred to as power *bases*, or sometimes assets, frequently confuses the subject. It is largely responsible for the numerous power-like words, some of which were mentioned at the beginning of this unit. For example, if different authors at different times write about coercive force, or persuasive influence, or normative control, they are all writing about the same concept, power, but labelling it according to the resource bases that are used. Coercive force probably means that physical resources are used such as weapons or prison walls; persuasive influence probably means that special knowledge or expertise, or the implication of it, are used to back verbal pressure; normative control probably means that an ideological attraction is the supporting resource.

5.2 Classifications of resources
Read Etzioni's account of different types of power resources (1970). This classifies power as coercive (physical resources) or remunerative (material resources) or normative (symbolic resources). Some organizations emphasize one kind of resource, some another, though any one organization may use all kinds of resource.

Organizations relying mainly on physical force to affect behaviour are exemplified by prisons, concentration camps and custodial mental hospitals. Material resources are the primary means for business, commercial, administrative and industrial organizations which reward their members with income and fringe benefits. Symbolic resources are rituals or objects which act as symbols of love, esteem, or prestige as in religious and sometimes in political organizations, universities or colleges, and voluntary associations. Etzioni suggests that this last could also be called persuasive or suggestive power.

Thus bureaucracies, for example, are not all identical. They differ sharply in the primacy of resources legitimately used for control under their bureaucratic rules and hierarchy. A bureaucracy may rely more on coercive power (a prison) or on remunerative power (a factory or bank) or normative power (a hospital).

Attractive though Etzioni's analysis is, it has been very little tested empirically. Hall *et al.* (1967) made one attempt to do so, an attempt whose adequacy is challenged by Weldon (1972). Nothing can be said about the *degree* to which organizations differ in this way. And is this simple classification exhaustive or not?

A similar analysis put forward by French and Raven (1959) has been used more often for research purposes, but rarely to explore differences between organizations as such (for example, inconclusive results are reported by Bachman *et al.* 1968).

French and Raven's classification

French and Raven view power from the standpoint of the member of an organization who is subject to it. They suggest that superior levels – supervisors and managers of all kinds – use any or all of the following bases of power:

Coercive : the individual conforms because he believes he will otherwise suffer negative consequences, punishment.

Reward : the individual believes he will benefit if he conforms.

Referent : the individual is attracted to and identified with another, and so conforms to his desires.

Expert : the individual believes that another has superior knowledge or expertise to which he defers.

Legitimate : the individual accepts the right of another to power over him.

So a supervisor can have an employee's pay withheld for late attendance, or allocate him the most troublesome work, i.e. use coercive power. Or a supervisor can recommend a pay increase, i.e. reward power. If the supervisor is personally admired by his subordinate then he can successfully ask for extra work, i.e. referent power. Should the supervisor be known for his skill at the job then a subordinate will accept his instruction as expert power. In addition if a subordinate conforms because he believes that it is in some sense 'right' to do so, or in the proper order of things, then the basis of power is called 'legitimate'.

Comparison of the two typologies

These five bases resemble Etzioni's categories, though his are meant to show broad differences between organizations whereas French and Raven imply that within any one organization individuals may differ in their reasons for complying. French and Raven's coercive power includes Etzioni's physical coercion, but extends also to the negative aspect of his remunerative power: reward power and remunerative power appear to match: referent power matches Etzioni's normative or identitive power, and expert power may also come within the normative category.

Legitimacy is treated differently, however. In Etzioni's scheme, coercive, remunerative, or normative power may each be used legitimately or non-legitimately or in some degree legitimately. In this light, the listing of legitimacy among the bases of power by French and Raven is confusing, even mistaken. Legitimacy is not an exclusive category of power base, but a variable quality of each of the other bases. For example, coercion can be legitimate (the control of deserters in an army) or non-legitimate (physical brutality to factory workers); expertise can be legitimate (the chief accountant's decision on a budgeting problem) or non-legitimate (the physics professor's attempt to tell sociology lecturers how to teach). And Weber's authority of office (based on the *reward* systems of the organization) and authority of expertise (the *expert* base) are both legitimate (Units 4/5).

Before considering legitimacy any more, we should look briefly at dependence.

5.3 Exchange and dependence

Dahl, a foremost student of power in the wider community setting, writes: '. . . power terms in modern social science refer to subsets of relations among social units such that behaviours of one or more units (the responsive units) depend in some circumstances on the behaviour of other units (the controlling units).' (1968 p. 407.) Emerson has formulated this idea of dependence explicitly: 'The dependence of actor A upon actor B is (1) directly proportional to A's motivational investment in goals mediated by B, and (2) inversely proportional to the availability of those goals to A outside of the A–B relation.' (1962 p. 32.) That is, B depends on A to the extent that he can only get what he wants from A or via A. Dependence, then, is a concept which analyses the balance of desired resources in a way which overlaps with economic theory on demand and supply.

Applying this to organizations, March and Simon (1958) analyse how an individual decides to join an organization in the first place (his 'decision to participate') and is then motivated once he has joined. The organization is seen as an exchange system in which inducements (or resources) are handed out in exchange for contributions given. Members are dependent on the organization for income, for status, for opportunities for personal achievement, and for the security of all these (summarized in Dunkerley 1972 p. 46).

Similarly, Blau and Scott's (1963) classification of organizations by who is the 'prime beneficiary' (*not* sole beneficiary) of their existence (see Dunkerley 1972 p. 59) emphasizes what the various groups connected with organizations contribute in return for benefits. They provide capital, or labour, or the purchase price for outputs, or legitimation for the organization's continued operation in society, and the organization dependent upon these resources must give adequate recompense.

6 Responses (or 'effects')

6.1 Member compliance

So organizations depend on their members and their members depend on them. Which brings us to the other aspect of our definition of power: *effect* upon others. How are the members affected, how do they respond?

Over this there is a fundamental obscurity in analyses of power, arising from the empirical difficulty, even impossibility, of distinguishing responses to someone's power (or to an organization's or sub-unit's power) from responses to everything else that happens.

However, Etzioni's typology again offers a sweeping perspective, untested though it is (Dunkerley 1972 p. 60). His typical and 'congruent' cases 1, 5 and 9, hypothesize that the use of coercion brings an alienative response, the use of remuneration in the widest sense of that word brings a calculative response, and the use of normative bases brings a moral response. On the face of it, this is appealing. People who are coerced don't like it, people who are paid do count the cost, and people who are offered ideological aims do morally commit themselves. Of course, most cases are mixed, as the other typology categories suggest: hospital staffs have gone on strike for more pay when the normative power of appeals to their moral commitment has waned, and armies have been led by highly paid foreigners though they themselves have been expected to give more in patriotism than they got in cash.

Alienation, of course, is frequently used as a wider concept which would include both Etzioni's alienative and calculative categories of compliance. It is seen as an effect of power, or rather of powerlessness. Those whose sole resource is their labour and expertise, and who do not have the power that goes with the control of the capital and technology resources of organizations, are regarded as alienated from or non-involved in the organizations and societies to which they nominally belong (and see again the discussion in Unit 1).

Etzioni's three kinds of power produce congruent responses:
coercive ⟶ alienative
remunerative ⟶ calculative
normative ⟶ moral

SAQ 7 Can you name one of Etzioni's 'non-congruent' cases, where the resource emphasized would not match member involvement?

A wider concept of alienation

SAQ 8 What is the purpose of analysing organizations in terms of resources?

6.2 Legitimacy

As you may have thought when reading Section 5.2, the classifications of resources by Etzioni and by French and Raven can give some illumination of the constant conflicts in all societies over the rightful – legitimate – use of power. In Britain, for example, the potential coercive resources of business organizations are questioned, as trained security guards multiply to guard factories and to guard money. Equally, the pressures put by trade union members on their fellows to come out or stay out on strike are regarded suspiciously. Thus the use of coercive power is the most carefully watched and defined, though, as was said earlier, there are always differing views on the legitimacy of power. Strikers dealing rather forcefully with blacklegs may not see coercion in the same light as do the journalists who write about it.

As with coercive power so too the legitimacy of reward power is limited: nothing 'smells worse' than the over use of rewards (e.g. money). Likewise, the exploitation of someone else's devoted loyalty (i.e. wrong use of referent power) may be frowned on; and so might be the use of moral commitment to minimize wage costs, such as low pay in hospitals (i.e. wrong use of normative power).

Until now this unit has taken for granted the existence of organizations as power systems more or less legitimated by the societies of which they are an integral part. Organizations yield these societies benefits which range from wealth to health. The legitimation which they are accorded approves their use of resources such as capital, which they may have a right to own, and certainly to use, or information which they may retain as trade secrets or patents, and so on. It also approves their hierarchical power because of its charismatic, traditionalistic, or rational-legal sources (Weber: see Unit 1).

This is not to imply that the acquisition of power-full resources by organizations goes unquestioned. In most if not all 'organizational societies' there are groups, large or small, blatant or concealed, which deny the legitimacy of the use of resources by certain organizations. In Europe or North America there are histories of demonstrations against the scientific development of weapons, or mining in scenic countryside. Unit 2 refers to fears that the powers of multinational corporations may exceed the power of any one state to control their activities. Their vast yet dispersed economic assets might enable them to make investment and price decisions which affect economic trends and employment in countries which have no influence on those decisions. There are also less conspicuous organizations legitimated only by some sections of a society, for example clandestine presses or resistance fighters/terrorists.

So there is no such thing as legitimate power in an absolute sense. There is continual conflict in societies and in organizations over what resources can be legitimately used in which way for what. That is, legitimacy of the weight, scope, and domain of power is a matter of degree and a matter of who sees it that way and who does not. Compliance with power is not only a matter of being dependent and having little choice, but is also affected by whether that power is felt to be rightfully exercised. Moreover, the legitimacy of the power of organizations and the power in organizations is inevitably partly defined by organizations, in the process of negotiating their own rightfulness and acceptance (see Units 7 and 9 on negotiated order and rules). They lobby, they have representatives on committees and commissions public and private, they advertise, they wine and dine, they improve working conditions; and from such activity flows their own legitimacy.

Section 2 of this unit discussed hierarchical power, and indicated that its distribution differs in different organizations. Those with some 'voluntary' (non-paid) membership can even appear to have an inverted hierarchy in which the membership is perceived as having more influence than the officials. This is probably a characteristic of many organizations which rely heavily upon a normative power base to obtain a moral or ideological commitment. Particularly when democratic values form part of this commitment, as they usually do in trades unions or political parties, there is pressure to limit hierarchical power (a completely egalitarian control graph would be a level line).

Something similar occurs in organizations with members who are trained in highly professionalized occupations. They also rely on normative power, or in French and Raven's terms, referent and expert bases. For example, Warren (1968) found that in American schools with more highly professionally orientated teachers, legitimate (treated separately), expert, and referent power bases are emphasized more than

The denial of legitimacy

Legitimacy is limited and conditional

Legitimacy is negotiated

Opposition to hierarchy

coercive and reward power. In such organizations (universities, colleges, hospitals, libraries, research departments of companies, etc., in whole or in part) the professionalized members respond to the aims of the organization and look up to others because of their superior professional expertise, and are comparatively (stress comparatively) less concerned with remunerative power than are the members of most business organizations. Such power is more covert, less overt, as Unit 1 has argued.

SAQ 9 Taking factories in your society, what power do you consider legitimate? That of their owners? Of managers? Of medical experts? Of government officials over them? Of trades unions?

7 Some problems and variables

7.1 Dependence, and omnipresent power

The examination of power in organizations in this unit has many of the features of the wider literature on this vexed topic. One such feature is its inclusion of the concept of dependence. Up to a point, dependence is useful in explaining power processes in the organizational setting. It fits easily enough the idea of having to rely on others for remuneration or for their superior expertise or for ideological inspiration. But the idea of depending on others for coercion is rather strained. There are at least two ways of resolving this difficulty. One is to extend the conceptualization of dependence so that it is thought of as a rewards and punishments model of behaviour. Then power resources are seen as rewards or punishments (coercion the latter) and responses are ranged from positive to negative. Many discussions of power implicitly assume this model. Another way might be to tighten the definition of an organization so that anyone who was coerced would be regarded as outside it, and not 'involved' with it in Etzioni's sense of the word.

Dependence and coercion don't fit together

Alternative 1: rewards and punishments model

Alternative 2: redefine organization to exclude the coerced

A further aspect of the literature on power is that it tends to treat power holders and their access to resources as being distinct from power subjects and their responses, so risking an implication that power subjects – which means everyone – are somehow free agents voluntaristically entering or avoiding dependence relations with others. Although this raises the whole issue of 'free will' versus 'oversocialized man' which pervades social analysis, that issue will have to go begging for an answer here, but at least let it be stressed again that any individual, group, organizational sub-unit or organization, indeed any social sub-system, is part of an encompassing social system that has an unequal distribution of power. No 'power incident' in an organization is enacted on a blank sheet, for even if the power structure should not be known to the particular participants, it is communicated and constructed as soon as interaction occurs.

7.2 Invisible power

Yet even though power may be omnipresent, it is not necessarily self-evident. This is a major obstacle to empirical research which finds power difficult or impossible to observe, yet at the same time finds it almost equally difficult to obtain adequate reports of power from participants who experience it. For instance, on the face of it power may seem obvious enough in union-management negotiations. On each issue raised, from the rate of pay per hour to number of hours worked, the power balance might be detected. But even if it could be, what then of those issues *not* raised? Power will also have played a part in determining that the union will not raise issues which directly question the right to supervise, nor management raise issues which directly question the right to strike. In short, there are everywhere in organizations unspoken issues from the trivial to the revolutionary, the 'unspokenness' of which is itself evidence of power. Not only are decisions the outcome of power processes, so are non-decisions.

Power determines what issues are not raised

More than that, Silverman (1970 chapter 6) emphasizes that the meaning in language itself is evidence of power. Suppose that a university staff group proposes to a committee that a new course on 'Organizations' be offered. It could be that in the

Power and language

university many people think of sociology as a 'soft' subject and of sociologists as 'unreliable', whereas management is 'hardheaded' and 'sound'. If so, the first issue is not the proposed course itself, but the word(s) by which it will be known and the associated language in which it will be discussed and hence the concepts by which it will be construed. Should the course be called 'Organizational Sociology' its fate may be different than if it is called 'Organizational Analysis', or if (irrespective of its title) it is discussed as an exercise in theoretical sociology rather than as a contribution to practical management. The several interest groups concerned may spend more effort on the 'language issue' than on the substantive syllabus. In such ways the whole 'language' of an organization becomes an indication of its power structure, from its 'cost consciousness' (or its 'cheese-paring') to its 'personal initiative' (or its 'rat race'); with its 'bosses', 'pay packets' and 'absenteeism'.

'Let's call it a management course'

This is a major factor in the complexity and protractedness of many of the decision processes mentioned earlier.

SAQ 10 What problems are there in distinguishing the powerful and those subject to their power?

7.3 Some variables linked to power

Hickson *et al.* write:

> Typically, research designs have treated power as the independent variable. Power has been used in community studies to explain decisions on community programmes, on resource allocation, and on voting behaviour; in small groups it has been used to explain decision making; and it has been used to explain morale and alienation. But within work organizations, power itself has not been explained. (Hickson *et al.* 1973 p. 174.)

It may be so that there is no coherent theory, but this unit has tried to construct a framework for understanding, and several useful concepts have recurred in it.

One is the concept of sole control of resources, or monopoly, or being irreplaceable or exclusive and unique, or as Hickson *et al.* (1973 pp. 181-2) term it, *(non)-substitutability*. Here is a concept common to sociology and economics. Mechanic (1962) is one of the few authors to have stated plainly what it means in an organization. In all organizations, superiors are inclined to see themselves as having more power over subordinates than subordinates see them as having (look again at the control graph in Figure 2). Subordinates come to know their own jobs better than their superiors know these jobs, and so, Mechanic argues, superiors then have to depend on their subordinates' expertise and the latter gain power as a result. This necessarily assumes that superiors cannot get the job done in any other way because the subordinates are non-substitutable (see also Emerson's definition of dependence at the beginning of Section 5.3 of this unit). Michels (1949) shows the same tendency working in the opposite direction. Because the officers of voluntary-membership organizations acquire experience and skill in leadership and administration which other members do not get, they become a powerful self-perpetuating oligarchy; and this tendency is presumably present in all organizations, something which applies to managers as much as to union officials (see Michels 1970).

Either way, the crux of the matter is non-substitutability of 'expertise', using that word in its widest meaning.

Related to substitutability is the concept of *uncertainty*. Crozier (1964) brought home what it might mean for power when he concluded that in small French tobacco manufacturing plants the maintenance engineers were powerful because 'machine stoppages are the only major happenings that cannot be predicted'. (Crozier 1964 p. 109.) Therefore the engineers had 'control over the last source of uncertainty remaining in a completely routinized organizational system' (p. 109). In short, all ran smoothly except for uncertain machine breakdowns, and the engineers had power because they knew what to do. This is a perspective taken from the view of organizations as open systems in uncertain situations (Unit 6).

Non-substitutability

Interdependence and the power of subordinates

Uncertainty

Another critical concept for the understanding of power is the *goals* and hence the task priorities of an organization. Its goals are both decided by power, and also shape power consequently. For example, Zald (1962) interpreted the loss of power by 'custodial' staff in correctional institutions as being due to a shift in the goals of such institutions from merely shutting up offenders to the treatment of their problems. So treatment-oriented staff became more influential.

Goals

Bringing together these concepts of substitutability, uncertainty, and goals, it would be possible to argue that those who can offer to organizations resources (e.g. expertise) which cope with uncertainties that the organization's goals define as important, and for which the organizations have no substitute, will have power in and over those organizations. Since power can be self-sustaining if it is used to control resources which confer more power, it may be possible for those who cope with uncertainty simultaneously to influence the organization's goals in favour of their own power position. Marketing experts who know how to sell in a particular market may be powerful enough to sway production decisions so that the firm continues to produce for that market. Hence the marketing director becomes the next managing director, and a 'sales-dominated' firm is perpetuated. In recent years some British industries have been criticized as being 'production-dominated' in this way. Similarly, those who meet financial uncertainty by supplying capital may be able to preserve their own position indefinitely.

Now read Hickson *et al.*'s account of a 'strategic contingencies theory' of intra-organizational power which brings these concepts together. (1973 pp. 174–89.) This theory offers an explanation of the differences in power between sub-units which were described in Section 3 of this unit. Though these authors apply the theory only to sub-units, the ideas on which they are drawing have a much wider currency in the socio-institutional 'market' in which power resides, and in which organizations play a salient part.

SAQ 11 Can you improve on your and our first answer to SAQ 5?

These concepts help to move the study of organizational power away from speculation about the power motives of specific groups in an organization (such as managers, or owners, or officials). Whilst such groups may indulge themselves in the pursuit of a variety of objectives they can only do so in the long run in relation to the socio-economic situation. As Blackburn notes about managers in business:

> The motives behind the decision of a manager may well be very complex and seemingly removed from economic calculations: he may desire to impress his wife or secretary, to further a personal vendetta, etc. But, finally all these aims, by a sort of reduction of quality to quantity, will have to be mediated by the market; managerial decisions will have to be vindicated in market terms, as failure within the market will frustrate almost every kind of ambition and, indeed, threaten to deprive the manager of his managerial functions. (Blackburn 1972 p. 170.)

7.4 Some views of power

There are many ways of shelling an egg, and there could be as many ways of looking at power in organizations. The unit you have just read is therefore inadequate by definition: and your aim must be to formulate your own judgements. One cheerful thought is that, though you will never get everyone to agree you are right, neither will they agree you are wrong!

For example, from one point of view, power is distributed 'up and down' organizations, but mainly 'up'. This is reflected in Section 2 on hierarchical power. So Parkin summarizes Dahrendorf's view that 'every single large scale organization has a dominant and subordinate class; administration and students in university, clergy and laity in the church, warders and inmates in prison, managers and workers in factories, and so forth.' (1971 pp. 45–6.) The dominant group forms an elite of powerholders and their associates. Its dominant power is because it has the capacity to

Rulers and ruled

use those resources which have the most weight over the domain and scope at issue. It may own the capital under capitalism, or have the party memberships which confer reward and referent power under communism, or whatever. It may have the special skills denoted by Michels' 'iron law of oligarchy'.

However, this elitist perspective does not necessarily mean that total power is with the elite. Mechanic's case for the power of subordinates has been discussed above in relation to Michels'. Subordinates too have know-how. Further, they can band together to exercise their power in the form of massed labour resources. Collective action by underdogs, whether workers, or middle managers facing a crisis together, or firms resisting government pressure, adds the power of one to the power of all and brings 'strength in numbers', not least because it makes each one less substitutable.

From another point of view, power is distributed 'here and there' around organizations. This is partly reflected in Section 3 on sub-unit power, and in Blau and Scott's classification of the groups who benefit from organizations. Owners, customers, suppliers, government legislators and public officials, trade unionists, competitors, associated organizations or agencies, consultants – are there more? – all play a part in the life of an organization, as do its internal sub-units, its managers, and its subordinate clerks, workers, or whatever. All of these also have power in the life of an organization, because of the part they play. There is a plurality of powerholders, when seen from this pluralist perspective.

So are organizations tools for control in the hands of those who set them up or hold most power? Are they coalitions between powerful sections or interests? Are they collaborative entities in which power is dispersed for the common aim? Well what are they?

Pluralist perspective

Answers to self-assessment questions

Answer SAQ 1
The concepts of 'organization' and 'power' tend to be inseparable. It is impossible to think of an organization without assuming something about human actions directed towards some end, and being related in particular ways to one another with respect to that end. The concept of power deals with how these actions are tied together; for example, through some people *intending* it, and because they have usable *resources* to which others respond. Organizations are power systems.

Answer SAQ 2
Hierarchy is the differential distribution of power among the members of organizations. Power is distributed in such a way that some who occupy certain positions or offices have more than those in other positions, so that an organization is seen as a hierarchy with the more powerful few at the 'top'. Their power coordinates and controls those 'below', so that hierarchy is also a division of labour with those 'above' doing the managing and administrating.

Answer SAQ 3a
Pugh and Hickson measure formal decision making authority; Tannenbaum measures an overall assessment by organization members of the process of influence.

Answer SAQ 3b
Pugh and Hickson do not cover the intricate process of intergroup and interpersonal power which surrounds formal authority. Many who do not officially take decisions may play a part in the process of decision. Tannenbaum may pick up general impressions of power formed by people who are aware of this process, but it is impossible to know exactly what people do mean by their answers to general questions on influ-

ence. Neither Pugh and Hickson nor Tannenbaum cover the control of the organization and its assets which sets the pattern(s) of power that they trace.

Answer SAQ 4

Accounting and Engineering, if only their overall mean scores of 2.7 are used. But Accounting has high power on all three Personnel issues as well as in the Finance area, and perhaps this is a subtlety which should be weighed in the balance. The measurement of power is complex, and any particular data may have only limited meaning.

Answer SAQ 5

This question is raised more directly at the end of this unit. But there are already some clues as to the possibilities.

Sub-units appear to do best when they deal with something which varies, as when buyers get a variety of supplies (Strauss); or when they have a special skill and central position (Hinings et al.); or when they have the know-how to deal with unpredictable problems (Crozier); or when they have to deal with resources which become scarce (Landsberger).

Answer SAQ 6

Any process in organizations which involves the generation or allocation of resources is a decision, and where human actions are affected it is part of a power process. But power processes also determine what issues are considered for 'decision making' (Normann and Carter), and lay down the normative rules determining which problems must be confronted (Cohen et al.). The making of decisions should not be thought of in isolation from the shaping of decisions.

Answer SAQ 7

For example, box 6 (e.g. a factory appealing normatively for extra work without more pay), box 8 (e.g. a monastery stressing its high standard of living accommodation to attract recruits). (They can be found in Etzioni 1970 p. 108.)

Answer SAQ 8

To try and explain better why groups and individuals do as others direct. The difficulty is the complexity. Any one organization may use all these kinds of resources, as may any one 'boss' in an organization, e.g. the well-informed and able supervisor (expert power) who encourages subordinates by recommending a rise in pay for them (reward power), an act which reflects his generous personality (referent power). Any one employee may respond to all resources, e.g. the airline pilot who likes his high pay *and* believes he is doing a public service *and* respects his boss. The link between resource and (others') response is unclear: the suggested consistency of emphasis in different organizations remains a hypothesis.

Answer SAQ 9

This is a vexed problem, philosophical and political as well as sociological. One commentator has posed it in this way:

> (The theorist) . . . may be struck by the seeming arbitrariness or conventionality of human authority: how is it that some men have the right to command, and others are obligated to obey? And so the theorist looks for the general difference between legitimate authority on the one hand, and illegitimate, naked coercive force on the other. He begins to wonder whether there is really any difference in principle between a legitimate government and a highway robber, pirate or slave-owner. He begins to suspect that terms like 'legitimate', 'authority', 'obligation' may be parts of an elaborate social swindle, used to clothe those highway robbers who have the approval of society, with a deceptive mantle of moralistic sanctity. Essentially, he begins to ask whether men are ever truly obligated to obey, or only coerced. (Pitkin 1972 p. 47.)

This is one point of view: what do you think?

Answer SAQ 10

The conceptualizing of distinct units, groups, or people as separate elements in a power relationship can be misleading. They do not exist in a social vacuum. Thus Section 5.3 has said that it is possible to distinguish A from B by saying that A is the more powerful because B is *dependent* on him for certain things. But taken by itself this is inadequate for there will be a third party(ies) C who has laid down the rules within which B is dependent on A. Clearly, we would not wish to attribute the 'power' of a foreman over workers solely to the *foreman*, but rather to the wider organizational power system within which he is a foreman. The encompassing social system is always there.

A further problem can be the obscurity of power, which means that even if we can identify those 'subject to power' we may not be able to identify the powerful. One is reminded of a farmer in *The Grapes of Wrath* who was in no position to know who was responsible for the confiscation of his land. Nor, apparently, was anyone else!

Answer SAQ 11

Sub-units or departments are within organizations and societies which determine their existence and rule what they may do. They have resources of money, equipment, information, and of people and skills, which may be used for their activities. If we take Hickson *et al.*'s concepts to synthesize the examples from SAQ 5, we can hypothesize that a sub-unit which uses its resources to *cope with an uncertainty* for the wider organization power system, and is positioned *centrally* in that system so that others are dependent upon it, and for which those others can find *no substitute*, will gain power. That is, a sales department which gets in steady orders despite a fluctuating market, so allowing the rest of the company to continue working smoothly, gains power, expecially if no sales consultants are available who might do the same job – but there are moral and legal limits to what it may do to get these orders, and in using its power in the company there may be limits to the expansion of its budget and staff at the expense of others. The power of each is constrained by the power of all.

References

BACHMAN, J. G., BOWERS, D. G. and MARCUS, P. M. (1968) 'Bases of Supervisory Power: A Comparative Study in Five Organizational Settings' in TANNENBAUM, A. (ed) *Control in Organizations*, New York, McGraw Hill, pp. 229–38.

BACHRACH, P. and BARATZ, M. S. (1962) 'Two Faces of Power' in *American Political Science Review*, LVI, 4, pp. 947–52.

BIERSTADT, R. (1950) 'An Analysis of Social Power' in *American Sociological Review*, 15, pp. 730–6.

BLACKBURN, R. (1972) 'The New Capitalism' in BLACKBURN, R. (ed) *Ideology and Social Science*, London, Fontana, pp. 164–86.

BLAU, P. and SCHOENHERR, R. A. (1973) 'New Forms of Power' in SALAMAN and THOMPSON (eds) pp. 13–24.

BLAU, P. and SCOTT, W. R. (1963) *Formal Organizations*, London, Routledge and Kegan Paul.

CARTER, E. E. (1971) 'The Behavioural Theory of the Firm and Top-Level Corporate Decisions' in *Administrative Science Quarterly*, 16, 4, pp. 413–29.

CARTWRIGHT, D. (1965) 'Influence, Leadership, Control' in MARCH, J. G. (ed) *Handbook of Organizations*, Chicago, Rand McNally, pp. 1–47.

CHILD, J. (1973) 'Organizational Structure, Environment and Performance: The Role of Strategic Choice' in SALAMAN and THOMPSON (eds) pp. 91–107.

CLARK, B. R. (1956) 'Organizational Adaptation and Precarious Values: A Case Study' in *American Sociological Review*, 21, pp. 327–36.

COHEN, M. D., MARCH, J. G. and OLSEN, J. P. (1972) 'A Garbage Can Model of Organizational Choice' in *Administrative Science Quarterly*, 17, 1, pp. 1–25.

CROZIER, M. (1964) *The Bureaucratic Phenomenon*, London, Tavistock.

CYERT, R. M., SIMON, H. A. and TROW, D. B. (1956) 'Observation of a Business Decision' in *Journal of Business*, 29, pp. 237–48.

CYERT, R. M. and MARCH, J. G. (1963) *A Behavioural Theory of the Firm*, Englewood Cliffs, Prentice-Hall.

DAHL, R. A. (1968) 'Power' in SILLS, D. L. (ed) *International Encyclopaedia of Social Sciences*, Vol. 12, London, Macmillan, pp. 405–15.

DUNKERLEY, D. (1972) *The Study of Organizations*, London, Routledge and Kegan Paul.

EMERSON, R. E. (1962) 'Power-Dependence Relations' in *American Sociological Review*, Vol. 27, pp. 31–41.

ETZIONI, A. (1970) 'Compliance Theory' in GRUSKY and MILLER (eds) pp. 103–26.

FRENCH, J. R. P. and RAVEN, B. (1959) 'The Bases of Social Power' in CARTWRIGHT, D. (ed) *Studies in Social Power*, Ann Arbor: University of Michigan, Institute for Social Research, pp. 150–67.

GRUSKY, O. and MILLER, G. A. (eds) (1970) *The Sociology of Organizations: Basic Studies*, New York, The Free Press (set book).

GOFFMAN, E. (1968) *Asylums*, Harmondsworth, Penguin.

HALL, R. H., HAAS, E. J. and JOHNSON, N. J. (1967) 'An Examination of the Blau-Scott and Etzioni Typologies' in *Administrative Science Quarterly*, 12, pp. 118–39.

HININGS, C. R., HICKSON, D. J., PENNINGS, J. M. and SCHNECK, R. E. (1973) 'Structural Conditions of Intraorganizational Power' in *Administrative Science Quarterly* (to appear).

HICKSON, D. J., HININGS, C. R., LEE, C. A., SCHNECK, R. E. and PENNINGS, J. M. (1973) 'A Strategic Contingencies Theory of Intraorganizational Power' in SALAMAN and THOMPSON (eds) pp. 174–89.

KAPLAN, A. (1964) 'Power in Perspective' in KAHN, R. L. and BOULDING, E. (eds) *Power and Conflict in Organizations*, London, Tavistock, pp. 1–32.

KATZ, F. E. (1973) 'Integrative and Adaptive Uses of Autonomy: Worker Autonomy in Factories' in SALAMAN and THOMPSON (eds) pp. 190–204.

LANDSBERGER, H. A. (1961) 'The Horizontal Dimension in Bureaucracy' in *Administrative Science Quarterly*, 6, pp. 299–332.

LIKERT, R. (1961) *New Patterns of Management*, New York, McGraw Hill.

LINDBLOM, C. E. (1959) 'The Science of Muddling Through' in *Public Administration Review*, 19, pp. 79–88.

MARCH, J. G. (1955) 'An Introduction to the Theory and Measurement of Influence' in *American Political Science Review*, 49, pp. 431–50.

MARCH, J. G. (1957) 'Measurement Concepts in the Theory of Influence' in *Journal of Politics*, 19, pp. 202–26.

MARCH, J. G. and SIMON, H. A. (1958) *Organizations*, New York, Wiley.

MECHANIC, D. (1962) 'Sources of Power of Lower Participants in Complex Organizations' in *Administrative Science Quarterly*, 7, pp. 349–64.

MICHELS, R. (1949) *Political Parties*, Chicago, Free Press.

MICHELS, R. (1970) 'Oligarchy' in GRUSKY and MILLER (eds) pp. 25–43.

NORMANN, R. (1971) 'Organizational Innovativeness: Product Variation and Reorientation' in *Administrative Science Quarterly*, 16, 2, pp. 203–15.

PARKIN, F. (1971) *Class Inequality and Political Order*, London, MacGibbon and Kee.

PERROW, C. (1970) 'Departmental Power and Perspectives in Industrial Firms' in ZALD, M. (ed) *Power in Organizations*, Nashville, Vanderbilt University Press, pp. 59–89.

PETTIGREW, A. M. (1972) 'Information Control as a Power Resource' in *Sociology*, 6, 2, pp. 187–204.

PITKIN, H. (1972) 'Obligation and Consent' in LASLETT, P., RUNCIMAN, W. G. and SKINNER, Q. (eds) *Philosophy, Politics and Society* 4th Series, Oxford, Blackwell, pp. 45–85.

PUGH, D. S., HICKSON, D. J. and HININGS, C. R. (1968) 'Dimensions of Organization Structure' in *Administrative Science Quarterly*, 13, pp. 65–105.

PUGH, D. S. and HICKSON, D. J. (1973) 'The Comparative Study of Organizations' in SALAMAN and THOMPSON (eds) pp. 50–66.

ROY, D. F. (1973) 'Banana Time: Job Satisfaction and Informal Interaction' in SALAMAN and THOMPSON (eds) pp. 205–22.

SALAMAN, G. and THOMPSON, K. (eds) (1973) *People and Organizations*, London, Longmans (the Reader).

SILVERMAN, D. (1970) *The Theory of Organizations*, London, Heinemann (set book).

SIMON, H. A. (1947) *Administrative Behavior*, New York, Macmillan.

STRAUSS, G. (1962) 'Tactics of Lateral Relationship: the Purchasing Agent' in *Administrative Science Quarterly*, 7, pp. 161–86.

STRAUSS, G. (1963) 'Some Notes on Power Equalization' in LEAVITT, H. A. (ed) *The Social Science of Organizations*, Englewood Cliffs, Prentice-Hall, pp. 39–84.

TANNENBAUM, A. S. (1968) *Control in Organizations*, New York, McGraw Hill.

WARREN, D. I. (1968) 'Power, Visibility and Conformity in Formal Organizations' in *American Journal of Sociology*, 3, 6, pp. 951–70.

WELDON, P. D. (1972) 'An Examination of the Blau-Scott and Etzioni Typologies: A Critique' in *Administrative Science Quarterly*, 17, 1, pp. 76–8.

WHISLER, T. L., MEYER, H., BAUM, B. H. and SORENSEN, P. F. (1967) 'Centralization of Organizational Control: An Empirical Study of its Meaning and Measurement' in *Journal of Business*, 40, 1, pp. 10–26.

WRONG, D. H. (1968) 'Some Problems in Defining Social Power' in *American Journal of Sociology*, 73, pp. 673–81.

ZALD, M. (1962) 'Organizational Control Structures in Five Correctional Institutions' in *American Journal of Sociology*, 68, pp. 335–45.

Acknowledgements

Grateful acknowledgement is made to the following sources for material used in this unit:

Figures
Figure 1: National Panasonic (UK) Ltd for the Organization Chart from the Visitors Guide to the Matsushita Electronics Corporation; *Figure 2*: McGraw-Hill Book Company for Tannenbaum, *Control in Organization*. Copyright © 1968 by McGraw-Hill Book Company and used with their permission.

Tables
Table 1: D. J. Hickson, C. R. Hinings *et al.* for their article, 'Structural Conditions of Intraorganizational Power' (to appear in *Administrative Science Quarterly*).

Notes

Unit 4 Classification of organizations
Unit 5 Organization structure: the main elements and interrelationships
Graeme Salaman

Through the years, a man peoples a space with images of provinces, kingdoms, mountains, bays, ships, islands, fishes, rooms, tools, stars, horses and people. Shortly before his death he discovers that the patient labyrinth of lines traces the image of his own face. (Borges 1972 p. 174.)

But man is so partial to systems and abstract deduction that in order to justify his logic he is prepared to distort the truth intentionally . . .

Ah, gentlemen, what will have become of our wills when everything is graphs and arithmetic, and nothing is valid but two and two makes four? Two and two will make four without any will of mine! (Dostoyevsky 1972 p. 31 and p. 39.)

Nazi documents, captured after World War II, indicate that on the day Adolf Hitler committed suicide and Russian troops were marching through the streets of Berlin, officials of the Reichschancellery were too busy to look out of their windows. They were engaged in estimating and ordering paper clips for the next fiscal year. (Bensman and Rosenberg 1960 p. 189.)

Contents Units 4 and 5

Reading for these units

The reading for these units should be done in the following order. (For full references see References at the end of the units.)

1 Derek S. Pugh and David J. Hickson, 'The Comparative Study of Organizations' in Graeme Salaman and Kenneth Thompson (eds) *People and Organizations* (the Reader) pp. 50–66.

2 Sections 1 and 2 of 'Classification of organizations' and 'Organization structure: the main elements and interrelationships' (these units).

3 Peter M. Blau, 'The Comparative Study of Organizations' in Oscar Grusky and George A. Miller (eds) *The Sociology of Organizations* (set book) pp. 175–86.

4 Sections 3 and 4 of 'Classification of organizations' and 'Organization structure: the main elements and interrelationships' (these units).

5 Talcott Parsons, 'Social Systems' in Grusky and Miller (eds) pp. 75–82.

6 Section 5 of 'Classification of organizations' and 'Organization structure: the main elements and interrelationships' (these units).

7 Amitai Etzioni, 'Compliance Theory' in Grusky and Miller (eds) pp. 103–26.

8 Section 6 of 'Classification of organizations' and 'Organization structure: the main elements and interrelationships' (these units).

9 Joan Woodward, 'Technology and Organization' in Grusky and Miller (eds) pp. 273–90.

10 David L. Sills, 'Preserving Organizational Goals' in Grusky and Miller (eds) pp. 227–36.

11 Sections 7 and 8 of 'Classification of organizations' and 'Organization structure: the main elements and interrelationships' (these units).

12 John Child, 'Organizational Structure, Environment and Performance: The Role of Strategic Choice' in Salaman and Thompson (eds) pp. 91–107.

13 Chris Argyris, 'Peter Blau' in Salaman and Thompson (eds) pp. 76–90.

14 Sections 9 and 10 of 'Classification of organizations' and 'Organization structure: the main elements and interrelationships' (these units).

15 Arthur L. Stinchcombe, 'Bureaucratic and Craft Administration of Production' in Grusky and Miller (eds) pp. 261–72.

16 George A. Miller, 'Professionals in Bureaucracy: Alienation Among Industrial Scientists and Engineers' in Grusky and Miller (eds) pp. 503–16.

17 Richard H. Hall, 'Professionalization and Bureaucratization' in Salaman and Thompson (eds) pp. 120–33.

The following article is also relevant to these units although it is not essential reading.
   James D. Thompson and William J. McEwen, 'Organizational Goals and Environment: Goal-Setting as an Interaction Process' in Salaman and Thompson (eds) pp. 155–67.

Objectives of Units 4 and 5

The objectives of these units are as follows:

1 To discuss the reasons for studying organizations; to introduce students to the concept of organizational structure; and to continue and develop the theme of the previous unit by considering the mechanisms by which, and the ways in which, members of organizations are controlled or influenced by their employing organization.

2 To consider those issues and questions which are generally considered to be of interest, importance and significance by those who advocate or employ a structuralist approach. Two main issues will be considered: some organizational classifications that have been presented, and those factors that have been considered as significant determinants of organizational structures.

3 To continue the previous discussion of organizational power by introducing students to some of the work concerning the relationships between various aspects of organizational structure with particular reference (because of its thematic and theoretical centrality and practical significance) to different sorts of control structures and their consequences, or substitutes.

4 Throughout, attention will be paid to what are seen as difficulties and dangers that typically accompany (if they are not intrinsic to) the application and utilization of the structural analysis of organizations: namely that it can lead to a process of reification which results in what is held to be an observed correlation between various aspects of organizational structure being considered as evidence of a necessary, 'functionally imperative' relationship; and that the measurement of organizational structure itself is a highly problematic venture which can involve a confusion of regularity with intention.

5 Because of the way in which it is frequently used as a background resource in the definition and analysis of organizational structure the concept of organizational goal will be given particular critical attention; especially since so many of the classificatory schemes unquestioningly employ the concept in their schemes, or directly focus the classification on the goals of the organization or see these goals as in some way determinants of the organization's structure.

6 Finally, these units will attempt to demonstrate the relationship between practical considerations and issues – of our students and others – and academic sociology, although there will be occasions when this is only possible by adopting a rather critical perspective on what usually passes for organizational theory.

Introduction to Units 4 and 5

It is something of an orthodoxy in courses or books on organizations to begin with a statement of the importance of organizations, and hence of the need to study them. This assertion is often couched in terms of the multitude of ways in which, in our lives, we are involved in organizations, at birth, work, play, prayer, death and so on. Sometimes reference is made to the considerable benefits that are held to result from contemporary forms of organization – such as space, medical and academic research, or technological innovation in consumer industries, transport or communications.

Importance of organization

Traditionally, as Unit 1 discussed, sociological interest in organizations – or bureaucracies – centred upon the political significance of these phenomena. In particular the relation between bureaucratic forms of organization and democratic political processes (that is a concern for the interests of *all* members of society and for their involvement in political decision making) was addressed. It was also noted in Unit 1 that this issue preoccupied socialist theorists with an interest in the practical difficulties of achieving a socialist society. The essence of the problem has been succinctly put by Lenin in his summary of Engels' views: 'Engels emphasizes again and again that not only under a monarchy but *also in the democratic republic* the state remains a state, i.e. it retains its fundamental characteristic feature of transforming the officials, the "servants of society", its organs, into the *masters* of society.' (Lenin 1970 p. 91.)

Significance for political theory

This suggestion of the displacement of organizational goals and objectives – the replacement of an interest in serving the public (or the people in the case of a State bureaucracy) by a concern for the interests and advantages of those who belong to or lead the organization – will be considered again later in this unit, and will also reappear later in the course.

Organizations are also crucially important, it is argued (for example, in Unit 2) because of the size they sometimes attain and the possibilities for economic and political power that follow from this.[1] It has also been remarked that organizations can have political significance through the overlapping of those groups of persons who hold the top positions in government, economic, military and other organizations. Also the capacity of some organizations to mobilize and create support (and possibly finance) from the political sector and to 'stabilize', control and create their own economic and political environments, has been commented upon.

Power of organizations

Unit 2 also argued for an awareness of the extent to which organizations may be supplanting the nation state as new centres of world-wide power and control. Increasingly it is true to say that what happens in, say, Brazil is not unrelated to the fact that

> . . . in 1968 foreign capital controlled forty per cent of the nation's (Brazil's) capital market, sixty-two per cent of its foreign trade, eighty-two per cent of its maritime transport, 100 per cent of motor vehicle output, 100 per cent of tyre production, more than eighty per cent of the pharmaceutical industry, nearly fifty per cent of the chemical industry, fifty-nine per cent of machine production, sixty-two per cent of auto parts factories, forty-eight per cent of aluminium, ninety per cent of cement and seventy-seven per cent of the overseas airlines . . . half the foreign capital comes from the United States. (Clairmonte 1970, quoted in Chomsky 1971 p. 10.)

It has been argued that lying behind the anti-communist rhetoric of American foreign policy there lies a concern for obstructing independent economic development and opening sources of scarce raw materials, especially non-ferrous metals, and new

---

1 Consider the case of the American Department of Defense (DOD). This
 . . . system of military production and distribution . . . is the largest planned economy outside the Soviet Union. Its property . . . amounts to some $202 billion, or about 10% of the assets of the entire American economy. It owns 39 million acres of land; rules a population of 4.7 million direct employees or soldiers; and spends over $80 billion a year. This makes it richer than any small nation in the world, and of course incomparably more powerful. (Heilbroner 1970 p. 5.)

markets for multinational corporations. Furthermore, it has been argued that the Cold War attitudes and philosophies (and the far from cold Vietnam war) are highly advantageous to those American organizations that receive the $40 billion odd that the DOD spends every year in contracts. 'It is predictable, then, that opportunities to end the Cold War will be side-stepped, and that challenges to Cold War ideology will be bitterly resisted.' (Chomsky 1971 p. 24.)

Organizations, then, are important in practical, social and political ways. And for this reason it is crucial that those who claim an academic interest in describing and understanding the social world direct attention to these phenomena, which not only affect us directly in our separate capacities as employees, members, patients, clients or whatever, but also through their societal, political significance. But what, exactly, is it that should be studied about organizations? What is it that is problematical?[1] What needs to be explained? And how can they be investigated?

Essentials of organizational enquiry

It may already be clear that one issue does, typically, seem to be considered as the major problem to be addressed – that is, how is it that members of organizations behave, as a result of their membership of organizations, in the way that they do. What is it about membership of an organization that causes members to behave in ways that can be categorized as *organizational behaviour*? This question lies behind Engels' concern for servants becoming masters; it also inspires everyday 'lay' complaints about 'red tape' and bureaucratic (in the pejorative sense) behaviour.

The feeling is, then, that an organization involves, as a central and intrinsic element, some sort of controlling or influencing process which affects (or dominates) the behaviour of members. It is thus possible to speak, sensibly, of an organization; as against referring to the separate individuals who, as members, comprise it. The distinctive, and interesting, feature of organizations is that through exposing members to processes and procedures of control, they manage, it is claimed, to display a remarkable and observable degree of patterned, regular behaviour over time. And this regularity (or the fact that members are seen or considered to behave as organizational members, as bureaucrats of this or that sort, as salesmen, nurses or whatever) is called organizational structure, and is what enables organizations to be considered, studied and defined as discrete phenomena.

Now structure is of course a concept that is central to sociological discourse and enquiry, and sociology as an activity would be impossible without a concern for (or a commitment to) a view of social events as displaying ordered properties. But organizations, in contrast to other social phenomena, involve a deliberate, self-conscious concern for these ordered properties in as much as organizational structure is likely to be the subject of constant, ongoing, critical scrutiny (sometimes by persons who are professionally concerned with structural analysis and evaluation) with reference to the relationship between structure and the attainment of various desired objectives. For this reason structure is a concept that is particularly appealing to those who study organizations since it refers to not only the observer's (sociologist's) way of classifying and talking about what he claims to see in the social world, but is also a concept that is used and considered by those who are being studied – i.e. members of the organization.

Organizational structure

Structure as sociological and organizational concept

Essentially the concept organizational structure is used to refer to what is taken for the observed, patterned continuity in the behaviour and activities of organizational members over time. This regularity is, on the one hand, what is meant by organiza-

Definitions of organizational structure

1 Clearly there are many things that could be seen to be problematical about organizations (or anything else) depending on the approach used and the theoretical stance adopted. This question is considered here in the light of the earlier discussion of the social, political importance of organizations; that is, it is being asked: with reference to *a concern for the significance of organizations*, what needs to be explained? It will be clear that this enquiry is altogether different from the question: what is it that those who are professionally interested in organization theory have typically researched and studied in organizations? The difference between the answers to these two questions cannot but reflect badly on much of what passes for academic work on organizations.

tional structure, but is also held to be the *result* of the ways in which events, activities, responsibilities, authorities and so on are officially *structured* and controlled within and by the organization.[1]

The concept of structure has a long and impressive sociological pedigree. As noted it has been used to refer to the apparent existence of regularities (in societies, organizations and so on) in the behaviours and values of members which can be analysed without reference to the predispositions and decisions of those individuals. Thus Durkheim says there is, '. . . a category of facts with very distinctive characteristics: it consists of ways of acting, thinking and feeling, external to the individual, and endowed with a power of coercion by reason of which they control him.' (Durkheim 1938 p. 3.)[2] With reference to organizations the concept structure is used to refer to the uniform, standardized properties that may be discerned, for example the fact that some people (called salesmen) spend a lot of time attempting to sell (but not to manufacture or design) a variety of products that are produced by the company that employs them, while other employees spend their time performing a series of repetitive operations which, in combination, result in the manufacture of the finished product. Clearly there are a number of ways in which the structure of an organization can be considered: differences in task are just one; level of authority and type of function or product are others.

It will be clear that Weber too was interested in the structure of organizations, but his interest was directed not only towards organizational rules and procedures, and the ways in which tasks, responsibilities and duties are distributed and organized, but also towards understanding how it was that members were in fact controlled by these constraints; why people were prepared to behave in such ways as to produce a sense of organizational structure.

The notion of structure in analyses of organizations then typically involves two considerations: the existence (description, measurement) of regularities in the behaviour of members of the organization which clearly are related to their membership of the organization; and (at least implicitly) some reference to the ways in which these observed regularities are achieved. As is well known, sociologists tend to employ two main perspectives in viewing the problem of the origins of structure.[3] Simply, structure can be seen as an emergent feature of ongoing negotiations and interactions, or as a result of imposition and constraint.

It is worthwhile mentioning this distinction between processes that are held to produce the regularity and predictability that is meant by organizational structure and the regularity and orderliness itself, because research into and discussion of organizations has sometimes tended to confuse official definitions of what the organization is like with analysis of actual behaviours and events. That is, official attempts to create organizational structure (or descriptions and definitions of that structure) have been taken for descriptions of organizational structure even though it must be clear that they constitute only one of a number of possible determinants of actual behaviour, although of course a highly salient and important determinant.[4] This

Official descriptions of expected, or hoped for behaviour versus actual, observed events

1 This duality which often appears in utilizations of this concept reflects a long standing dichotomy in sociological studies of organizations between formal and informal structure, or between what is meant (designed) to happen and what actually happens. This distinction will be given considerable attention later in the course.

2 Blau puts it this way: 'The assumption implicit in this approach is that formal organizations, as well as other social structures, exhibit regularities that can be analysed in their own right, independent of any knowledge about the individual behaviour of their members.' (Blau and Schoenherr 1971 p. viii.)

3 These have been fully described and assessed elsewhere – The Open University (1972) D283 *The Sociological Perspective*, The Open University Press.

4 That rules, prescriptions, organization charts, job descriptions are problematically related to actual behaviour (in as much as the sense of a rule or whatever is only evident in the occasion of its use) is also highly relevant to this argument of the importance of separating attempts to determine organizational behaviour from actual events. This issue will be seriously considered later in the course, with reference to organizational rules.

distinction between official descriptions of the organizational structure and actual behaviours displayed by organizational members (and, presumably, observed by the sociologist) has serious methodological implications, since members of organizations themselves tend to perceive their jobs and activities in terms of their conception of what they *ought* to be doing. Burns' study of managers' estimates of their work activities showed that a manager's estimate was considerably affected by '. . . the assumptions (he had) about the context of organized activity in which his own work was being done'. (Burns 1967 p. 117.) This makes the description and analysis of organizational structure highly problematic since a number of different structures will be apparent, at least to those within the organization, who view it in terms of different priorities.

For many who study organizations the analysis and description (and understanding) of organizational structure constitutes the most interesting and important job.[1] Such an assertion is particularly attractive, in the case of organizations, because, as has been mentioned, organizations involve some degree of deliberate, self-conscious consideration and planning of their structures, of how things are, or should be, done. So Hall has written:

Organizational structure distinguished by its explicit design and construction

> . . . structure is actually more important to the understanding of what goes on in an organization than the particular individuals involved. While the activities of individuals are certainly an important input to organizations, the very nature of organizations is such that they are intended to minimize the influence of individual variations . . . Structural characteristics are an important consideration in understanding how an individual does react and behave in an organization. (Hall 1972a p. 10.)

Unit 4 Classification of organizations

1 Typologies of organizational structure

For reasons given above any consideration of organizations – or of the sociology of organizations – must be concerned with the structure of organizations. But is it possible to speak, generally, about organizations, as though they held characteristics in common? If membership of an organization means exposure to rules, procedures, job specifications and so on, are there different types of such control, of organizational structure, and if so how do they differ? And what causes these differences? In what ways are hospitals, prisons, commercial companies, churches and army camps similar?

Varieties of organizational structure

It will immediately be seen that such questions have considerable relevance and importance for those in senior positions within organizations who are concerned with the efficiency of the organization. For organizational structure will be seen by such members in terms of its appropriateness, its capacity to achieve what such people take for the goals of the organization. Thus Pugh and Hickson remark:

Relationship between structure and goals

---

1 Blau and Schoenherr, for example, see this as a necessary beginning to any attempt to control and regulate the potential power of organizations, and the threat to democracy they represent: 'Unless we take seriously the simple fact that organizations are not people, we as citizens shall not be able to meet this threat to democracy, and we as sociologists shall not be able to meet the main challenge our discipline poses.' (Blau and Schoenherr 1971 p. 357.) It is, however, only fair to add that others have argued that a concern for the structure of organizations restricts attention to the internal aspects at the expense of a sufficient interest in the social impact and consequences of large scale organizations.

All organizations have to make provision for continuing activities directed towards *the achievement of given aims*. Regularities in activities such as task allocation, supervision, and co-ordination are developed. Such regularities constitute the organization's structure, and the fact that these activities can be arranged in various ways means that organizations can have differing structures. (Pugh and Hickson 1973 p. 51. My emphasis.)

Unit 6 will consider organizations as systems, and it will note that systems can be of two sorts: open and closed. The closed system model sees the organization as a means designed to achieve the organization's goals.[1] All aspects of the organization's structure are, in this view, designed to achieve these goals. However, such a state of affairs is more easily described than attained. For not only are there all the difficulties surrounding the concept organizational goal, which are discussed later in this unit, and also contained in Silverman (1970), there is also the point that the closed system view involves a rather simple-minded conception of individual motivation and commitment to the organization (i.e. it overlooks the possibility that, and the extent to which, organizational members might see and pursue their own, sectional, interests rather than what they are told are the goals of the organization). But the main difficulty with the closed system model is that it ignores the ways in which the organization's 'rationality' (that is means-ends links) is affected – or reduced – through extra-organizational factors. The relevance of the open/closed system distinction to the subject matter of this unit is simply that inherent in the view of organization as open systems is the realization that the structure of an organization (for structure can be seen as the static aspect of a system) may be affected or determined by external factors. Such a view leads to the possibility that there may be different types of organizations depending on the environment they occur in.

It has been suggested that even Max Weber's work can be seen as referring to two sources of authority within bureaucratic organizations, authority based on incumbency of office, and authority based on expertise. Gouldner has argued, following this distinction that, empirically:

Gouldner's classification of organizational authority types

> . . . bureaucracy is not a single homogeneous entity but that there are two types of bureaucracy, the representative bureaucracy and the punishment-centred bureaucracy. The representative bureaucracy is, in part, characterized by authority based upon knowledge and expertise. It also entails collaborative or bilateral initiation of the organizational rules by the parties involved . . . The punishment-centred bureaucracy is characterized by authority based on incumbency in office, and by the unilateral initiation of organization rules which are enforced through punishments. (Gouldner 1959 p. 403.)

It is by no means established that this elegant distinction, which has been frequently used in analyses of the circumstances of professionals employed in large organizations, is valid. For one thing administration too demands expertise and knowledge; for another, as will be seen, it is very likely that the claimed incompatibility of professional (expert) and bureaucratic (incumbency in office) authority has been overstated.

But this distinction is only one of a number of different classifications of organizations that have been presented, criticized, ignored, rejected and utilized in the literature on organizations. That such a number of classificatory schemes exist is not surprising since the essence of these schemes is the suggestion that certain organizational characteristics tend to cluster together, to correlate, and organizational classification is thus closely related to the practical (managerial) task of finding and designing an organizational structure which is most *appropriate* for particular environments,

1 Unit 6 will also consider the notion of organizational goals and will point out some of the difficulties that attend the utilization of this concept in organizational analysis. In particular it will be remarked that organizational goals (say, profit) tend to be rather poor guides to actual actions or choices. This topic will also be considered later in these units. It would however be unfortunate if the impression was gained that the difficulties and disadvantages that accompany analyses of organizational structure in terms of organizational goals were here being overlooked, or glossed over.

technologies, personnel, etc. But it has also been suggested that a concern for classifying organizations is inherent in sociological conceptualization and theorizing about organizations, indeed in thinking on any subject. Hall has argued that 'Man must classify phenomena in order to be able to think about them. He must have some framework by which to view the world around him, or else he is surrounded by an unordered kaleidoscope of stimuli, rendering him unable to function at all.' (Hall 1972b pp. 39–40.)

Importance of classifications

The only way to assess the status and importance of a description or analysis of an organization is to compare it with descriptions, etc. of other organizations. But to do this we need to know whether all organizations are the same or whether there are different types. But we should be wary. Very frequently typologies of organizations tend to derive from a particular theoretical perspective (most notably in the case of Parsons) and be tenuously related to actual events and characteristics. Secondly they tend to oversimplify and to be based on a single characteristic which is held to be of importance in determining (or correlating with) other aspects of organizational structure and functioning. This leads to the really important point about organizational classifications – how useful are they in highlighting the key variables and key processes?[1]

Difficulties surrounding organizational classifications

In considering the three classificatory schemes outlined below two questions should be borne in mind, namely: what are the key differences between the organizational types? And what are the mechanisms or determinants that are held to produce these differences in organizational structure? These questions will be considered later on in these units.

2 Talcott Parsons

Parsons has applied his general theoretical framework to the analysis of organizations. And the results, predictably, are ambitious and idiosyncratic. As is well known Parsons' conception of the societal social system emphasizes the importance of four basic systemic problems, which societies (as systems) must resolve. These are:

1 *adaptation:* the accommodation of the system to the reality demands of the environment coupled with the active transformation of the external situation;
2 *goal achievement:* the defining of objectives and the mobilization of resources to attain them;
3 *integration:* establishing and organizing a set of relations among the member units of the system that serve to co-ordinate and unify them into a single entity;
4 *latency:* the maintenance over time of the system's motivational and cultural patterns. (Blau and Scott 1963 p. 38.)

For Parsons any system is made up of other systems. And he sees organizations as societal sub-systems which are mechanisms for achieving societal requirements, but which are also composed of sub-systems which attempt to resolve the organization's four basic system problems. (See above.) Analysis of organizations, for Parsons, is unequivocally part of '. . . the study of social structure' generally. (Parsons 1970 p. 75.) And organizations are defined in terms of their '. . . primacy of orientation to the attainment of a specific goal'. (Parsons 1970 p. 75.) This orientation has both internal and external organizational consequences. Internally the fact that organizations are goal-attaining systems has consequences for its 'special features', and '. . . gives priority to those processes most directly involved with the success or failure of

---

1 To quote Hall again:
The essence of the typological effort really lies in the determination of the critical variables for differentiating the phenomena under investigation . . . An adequate overall classification would have to take into account the array of external conditions, the total spectrum of actions and interactions within an organization, and the outcome of organizational behaviours. (Hall 1972b p. 41.)

goal-oriented endeavours'. (Parsons 1970 p. 76.) Externally Parsons' conceptualization of organizations in terms of their orientation towards the meeting of societal requirements and needs leads to a concern for and an interest in the ways in which organizational *products* (consumer goods, students, decisions) are used by other sub-systems within the society – sometimes other organizations, for example.

Organizations not only must address the same four problems as societies (and for this they will require specialized organizational departments or mechanisms), they can also themselves be categorized in terms of these four functional imperatives. Thus Parsons distinguishes four types of organization which he discriminates by reference to '. . . the type of goal or function about which they are organized'. (Parsons 1970 p. 80.) In this way Parsons arrives at a classification of the following four organizational types: economic organizations, political organizations, integrative organizations and pattern maintenance organizations.

Parsons' organizational types

A provocative and interesting feature of Parsons' approach to and view of organizations follows from his determination to consider them in terms of their functions for the larger, societal system. Parsons envisages organizations as ways of getting things done. This leads to an interesting and possibly misleading conception of power (which, presumably, is needed to get things done, as he would see it) as '. . . the generalized capacity to mobilize resources in the interest of attainment of a system goal'. (Parsons 1970 p. 79.) Such a definition seems to beg important questions that arise from the possibility that organizations may in fact pursue goals that could be seen as contrary to those of the society as a whole, and that within organizations different groups might hold very different conceptions of their interests, and the nature of the relationship between them. McMillan has argued, for example, in Unit 2, that multinational corporations are by no means concerned with national, societal goals; instead they can be seen as pursuing their own organizational interests (as these are seen and evaluated by policy-making personnel) as against the goals of their native society (whatever they might be).

Difficulties with Parsons' conception of relationship between organizational activities and society

Another surprising feature of the Parsonian view of organizations is that he sees organizational power as an allocation or grant, from the society to the goal attaining organization, and this is, therefore, a recognition and endorsement of the goals of the organization, and presumably of the means employed to attain them. Again such a view seems somewhat optimistic and, as will be seen, tends to lead to an excessive concern for certain sorts of organization and certain sorts of (stated, claimed) organizational goals.[1] As Silverman has remarked, such an approach would seem to overlook the existence of, for example, the Mafia. It also glosses over the real nature of organizational activities by accepting the *rhetoric* of organizations concerning their view of their goals.

Parsons' theoretical scheme is heavily oriented towards the legitimating importance of values. As has been noted, for example, he sees organizations as operating under a societal mandate, as it were, a grant or allocation of power which is given in order to achieve what are generally held to be legitimate organizational objectives, from the society's point of view. He writes: '. . . in more everyday terms, the goal of the society can be said to be to "get things done" which are approved in terms of its values as "worth doing" (the term "worth" may, of course, signify varying degrees of urgency).' (Parsons 1970 p. 79.) Once again this appears to be an extraordinarily optimistic (or naive) view, in face of what are taken to be everyday realities of organizations. The obvious possibility that organizations may seek to generate or utilize political or governmental power to seek the ends of senior and powerful organizational members seems to be defined away; as does the possibility that organizations ostensibly

Parsons' conception of necessary legitimacy of organizational activities and endeavours

---

1 At this stage the criticisms and anxieties about the Parsonian view will be only sketched in, since a fuller treatment of the most relevant and significant ones will be contained in the later section on organizational goals. But some mention of the more obvious difficulties must be made here in order to avoid the impression of implicitly condoning such an approach.

entrusted with the attainment of a societal goal (say the Pentagon's military activities in South East Asia) may deliberately withhold information from government personnel in order to pursue their own ends, or simply act in secret so as to create a *fait accompli*.[1] It has also been suggested that many organizations are simply too large, powerful and well equipped and staffed to bother about the nominal societal or governmental regulation. Once again a fuller discussion of this topic will occur later in these units.

Finally, without entering into the debate about what society's goals are, it is important to mention that the existence of some degree of legitimation for an organization (or a political party, or whatever) is not the end of the story. Anyone with an interest in understanding the dynamics and conflicts inherent in society (or an organization) will also wish to consider where these legitimations come from. In the area of organizational analysis this question is particularly important since organizations include as members, personnel (representing the senior members of the organization, or its owners) who will make strong, systematic and plausible efforts to justify the activity of the organization in terms of available and acceptable justifications or rhetorics. Thus hospitals (or Medical Associations) will, of course, claim to be concerned with the nation's health, and not the interests of doctors or the medical industry; and industry will be concerned with 'giving the customer what he wants', rather than maintaining the employment of managers. Thus, a value, goal, or symbol is invoked to justify actions which would seem to conflict with it. In this way the Orwellian situation can arise whereby, say, Vietnam is destroyed to 'make it free' (an available and generally acceptable motive and intention).

Organizational efforts to create or sustain their legitimacy

Apart from the difficulties mentioned above, Parsons' scheme is also vulnerable to the criticism that while it elegantly connects the study of organizations to a grandiose societal theory it actually fails to distinguish between organizations even in its own terms since it is extremely difficult (and possibly misleading) to allocate organizations to Parsons' categories, or to know what is an economic organization, or a political organization. And to use such classificatory categories directs attention away from the ways in which organizations that would assert, say, their economic aspects, have political ones as well. So again, really important and problematic social and political issues arising from the existence of organizations in society are simply ignored through the ways in which organizations – and societies – are theorized about and conceptualized. In this case the ways in which organizations have implications and objectives over and above those they claim and assert in their public relations pronouncements, their capacity to define and legitimize the nature of their activity and objectives, and interconnections between elite personnel and their interests in dominant positions in organizations that Parsons would consider to be different types, are simply not considered.[2]

Difficulties of classifying organizations by Parsons' criteria

1 A recent example of this sort of organizational behaviour has been furnished by the American Securities and Exchange Commission which has suggested that the gigantic International Telephone and Telegraph Corporation may have rewarded Vice-President Agnew for being instrumental in 'settling' a proposed anti-trust suit that ITT were facing by making large dollar 'gifts' to the Republican party. It has also been admitted by a senior official of the company that the company was involved in attempts to bring down President Allende's Marxist government in Chile by assisting in exacerbating economic crisis. After the election of President Allende in 1970 ITT and other giant corporations, including Ford and General Motors, established a committee which urged the White House to impose various sanctions and blockades on Chile. As a result of the findings of Senator Frank Church's sub-committee on multinational corporations, the *Guardian's* correspondent wrote: 'There is an uneasy feeling among legislators here that the multinational corporations of which ITT is a prime example, have in fact become political tools or even arms of the American Government'. (*Guardian* 21 March 1973.)

2 The extent of government involvement in business – through enormous government spending – has already been noted. But this is by no means all there is to the suggestion that the sorts of categories Parsons advocates are of limited utility. For example it has been stated that,

The intermingling of Big Military and Big Industry is evidenced in the 1,400 former officers working for the 100 corporations who received nearly all the $21 billion spent in procurement by the Defense Department in 1961. The overlap is most poignantly clear in the case of General Dynamics, the company which received the best 1961 contracts, employed the most retired officers (187) and is directed by a former secretary of the Army. (Students for a Democratic Society 1972 p. 16.)

But why bother with this consideration of Parsons' proposed organizational classification? There are three reasons, each deriving from the rationale of the course and these units. For one thing the somewhat extreme nature of the Parsonian classificatory scheme draws attention to the fact that organizations, or any other social phenomena, do not exist as unquestionable facts to be measured and described by the sociologist. Social phenomena are only apparent and available through the theories and concepts that are brought to bear on them. This point is made most emphatically with reference to the Parsonian scheme because, it is suggested, of its irrelevance to other, rather obvious, possibilities and considerations that are held to be apparent. But the existence and evaluation of these possibilities stems from the utilization of another, implicit, scheme.

Reasons for considering Parsons' scheme

Secondly, the Parsonian scheme is interesting because it is vulnerable for theoretical reasons. A few of the theoretical difficulties have been suggested above. A more thorough treatment is contained in Silverman (1970). The theoretical debate that revolves around Parsons' approach to organizations thus serves to emphasize that theoretical discussion is absolutely central to any consideration of social phenomena, no matter how pressing their practical significance.

Finally, the scheme considered above introduces an issue that will be allocated more attention later: the relationship between (what are claimed to be) the organization's goals and the structure of the organization. Another approach to organizational analysis and classification has been suggested by Etzioni. This scheme is outlined below.

SAQ 1 What are the main elements and criticisms of Parsons' classification of organizations?

3 Etzioni

Unlike Parsons, who sees organizational power as an unproblematic capacity allocated to organizations by 'society' with a view to attaining society's requirements or at least socially legitimate goals, Etzioni focuses on intra-organizational aspects of organizational power and control. For Etzioni, as for Weber, the interesting and significant feature of organizations is: '. . . why do people in organizations conform to the orders given to them and follow the standards of behaviour laid down for them?'. (Pugh *et al.* 1971 p. 30.)[1] Etzioni, like Parsons and others, argues strongly for the advantages of the comparative method. Such an approach requires a classificatory scheme. The scheme he offers involves, as he sees it, both motivational and structural elements. It is also firmly related to sociological thinking and discourse in other fields.

The key classificatory variable in the Etzioni scheme is *compliance*, which refers to the obedience of an organizational member (with respect to some command or rule) and the reasons for this obedience. Compliance is the result of two sorts of factors: the power means and the members' orientation towards (or involvement in) the organization's power system. Since Etzioni considers there are three sorts of power means (called coercive, remunerative and normative) and three sorts of involvement (alienative, calculative and moral) he necessarily argues for the theoretical possibility of nine compliance structures, although he maintains that in practice three types are found more frequently than the others. The reasons for this are interesting and will be considered later. It should however be noted that Etzioni's elegant combination of power and orientations in terms of each other has been described as tautologous. (Burns 1967.)

Etzioni's concern for compliance

Types of sanction and involvement

Etzioni maintains that classifying organizations by their compliance structures – that is, by whether they are utilitarian, normative or coercive organizations – is more useful than employing previous classifications. As he says:

---

1 Later units will argue that part of the answer to this question is that organizational members do not always (indeed cannot always) obey orders and regulations. But of course that does not imply that the degree of acquiescence and obedience that is achieved is unimportant.

The use of such common sense categories as labor unions and corporations to isolate the units of comparison creates considerable difficulty. This method of classification tends to attach the same label to organizations which differ considerably, and to assign different names to organizations which are analytically similar in many significant ways, particularly in their compliance structure. (Etzioni 1970 p. 112.)

Understandably Etzioni argues that his classification, which derives from sociological theory and from available work on organizations, is more useful, since it focuses upon what he considers as a key analytic attribute.

Using this variable, traditional organizational categories or types are subdivided. For example, Etzioni distinguishes between peacetime and combat units within 'military organizations'. Such a distinction is justified by the argument that peacetime and combat units display different compliance structures and so differ in various other significant respects. These associated variations are held to derive from the compliance variable. For example, Etzioni claims that organizational goals are related to compliance. ('Organizations that have similar compliance structures tend to have similar goals, and organizations that have similar goals tend to have similar compliance structures'. Etzioni 1961 p. 71.) Similarly, Etzioni argues that the way in which power is distributed within the organization is related to the compliance structure, for example coercive organizations involve a sharp distinction between inmates and officials, or rulers and ruled, but normative organizations emphasize the amalgamation or assimilation of *all* participants in the control process. Compliance is also related to the degree of cultural integration that exists within organizations. This last characteristic is considered with reference to three viewpoints, '. . . the degree of consensus between lower participants and organizational representatives on cultural orientations in a number of spheres; the symbolic processes reinforcing or modifying these orientations; and the processes introducing new participants to the culture of the organization and that of the lower participants' collectivities.' (Etzioni 1961 p. 149.) In support of Etzioni's claim for the predictive utility of his classificatory scheme he argues that coercive, utilitarian and normative organizations differ considerably in the degree to which reliance is placed upon normative agreement and commitment in order to achieve efficient operation. With respect to utilitarian organizations he argues that '. . . utilitarian organizations require consensus in those spheres which are directly related to instrumental activities – namely, cognitive, perspective, participation, and performance obligations.' (Etzioni 1961 p. 150.) This argument has added significance in the context of this course since not only is the subject of involvement and 'cultural integration' (or differentiation) one that is addressed by a number of writers in Salaman and Thompson (1973) (e.g. Turner, Roy and Fox) but the possibility of organizations controlling their personnel – or some of them – through trusting them to behave in accordance with the technical rationalities of their occupational or professional cultures, is a subject that is directly considered later in these units and is also a theme in the media contributions of this course.

Etzioni's classificatory scheme is interesting for our purposes not only because of the way in which it deliberately sets out to replace and reject what he classes as 'common sense' categories, such as military organizations, or unions, business organizations and so on, but also because it is directly concerned with organizational control, which is the central theme of this course. However it will be seen that Etzioni's scheme is also interesting for the way in which it raises two questions which will be discussed later, namely, how far is it empirically true that certain organizational characteristics tend to cluster around this (or any other) key classificatory variable, and if such empirical clusterings are discernible, then why do they come about? It has already been noted that for Etzioni the mechanism that produces what he claims to be the three most common organizational types (in terms of their compliance structure) is organizational efficiency.

Etzioni's application of the scheme

Interesting features of Etzioni's scheme

It has been sensibly argued that 'The essence of the typological effort really lies in the determination of the critical variables for differentiating the phenomena under investigation' (Hall 1972b p. 41), a sentiment with which both Parsons and Etzioni would agree. They would disagree, however, as the previous discussions revealed, as to *which* variables are critical in this context. It has been suggested that one obvious way to choose between the existing typologies is to discover, empirically, how organizations actually differ with respect to their structure. A study by Hall, Haas and Johnson (1967) found that although the theoretically derived classifications were helpful up to a point (that is as Hall reports, '. . . prisons were classified as "coercive" . . . and so on') (Hall 1972b p. 48), the applicability and relevance of these classifications was decidedly limited, not only with respect to the possibility of allocating an organization to one category or another, but also in terms of the determinate importance of the selected variable. With reference to what Hall takes to be significant features of organizational structure he concludes of the Etzioni classification that it has '. . . only a limited application insofar as total organizational analysis is concerned.' (Hall 1972b p. 51.)

Central features of the typological effort

The criticism that the theoretically derived classifications are empirically inaccurate and misleading, at least on occasion, and fail to pinpoint the organizational characteristic that empirically can be seen to correlate with (or determine) the form of the organizational structure (or those characteristics that are held to be generally important) leads us to consider the sorts of classification discussed below. This involves a significantly different approach from Parsons' and Etzioni's classifications and is worth serious consideration.

SAQ 2 Describe and evaluate Etzioni's classificatory scheme

4 Technology as a basis for classification: Woodward and Perrow

Woodward's classification of different types of organization grew out of an effort to investigate the applicability of the sorts of management principles that litter the management textbooks. Essentially the survey conducted under the auspices of this interest '. . . revealed considerable variations in the pattern of organization which could not be related to size of firm, type of industry, or business success.' (Woodward 1969 p. 196.)

However, Woodward continues, 'When the firms were grouped according to similarity of objectives and techniques of production, and classified in order of the technical complexity of their production systems, each production system was found to be associated with a characteristic pattern of organization.' (Woodward 1969 p. 196.) Three types of technology are isolated: small batch and unit production, large batch and mass production, and process production. These types are seen to differ with respect to technical complexity, which is defined as: '. . . the extent to which the production process is controllable and its results predictable.' (Woodward 1969 p. 203.) A number of organizational characteristics are seen to be related to the technical complexity of the work processes, for example, the number of levels of authority, the span of control of the first line supervisor, and the ratio of managers and supervisory staff to total personnel.

Woodward suggests technology as a determinant of organizational structure

Furthermore, Woodward claims that the relative importance of management specialist activities and the nature of their co-ordination and integration also varied with the technical system. For example, the nature of the technical process determined where the manufacturing cycle began – in unit production getting an order was the first step, whereas in mass production the goods were researched, developed and produced, and then sold. More specifically Woodward argues, on the basis of her findings, that a number of structural features are positively related to the degree of complexity of the production system. She remarks:

Structural characteristics Woodward maintains relate to technology

Among the organizational characteristics showing a direct relationship with technical advance were: the length of the line of command; the span of control of the chief executive; the percentage of total turnover allocated to the payment of wages and salaries, and the ratios of managers to total personnel, of clerical and administrative staff to manual workers, of direct to indirect labour, and of graduate to nongraduate supervision in production departments. (Woodward 1970 p. 279.)

Woodward's argument that technology determines organizational structure has been tested by Hickson *et al.* (1972). Using a more precise and specific notion of technology the authors found a complex and variable relationship between their findings and Woodward's; they write '. . . although a sweeping "technological imperative" hypothesis is not supported, a residual seven variables have been identified in the tests on manufacturing industry that do have associations with technology.' (Hickson *et al.* 1972 p. 148.) The crucial point about these features is that they are most directly concerned with the technology (e.g. variables like the proportion of personnel in maintenance, or inspection, which are obviously directly affected by the nature of the technology in a way that the proportion of personnel in accounting is not). The authors hypothesize that '. . . structural variables will be associated with operations technology only where they are centred on the workflow.' (Hickson *et al.* 1972 p. 150.) One corollary of this is that Woodward's findings would be most applicable to small firms.

Hickson *et al.'s* findings modify Woodward's conclusion

It is highly relevant to the overarching considerations of these units that Woodward, like Parsons and Etzioni, considers that the goals or objectives of the organization are, indirectly, important as determinants of organizational structure since '. . . differences in objectives controlled and limited the techniques of production that could be employed.' (Woodward 1969 p. 202.) Woodward also argues that if objectives give rise to differences in technology and thus, ultimately, to differences in organizational structure and process, then there '. . . can be no one best way of organizing a business.' (Woodward 1969 p. 202.) The optimum (from the point of view of efficiency) organizational structure must be seen not in terms of conformity with management principles, but in relation to the goals and technology of the enterprise. This view of organizational structure and some of its consequences is considered by Child (1973).

Woodward's findings have been most influential, and she is by no means alone in arguing that technology is an important determinant of organizational structure. Such a line has also been adopted by Perrow. Perrow sees organizations as phenomena within which things are done to raw materials of some sort. The things that are done – and the ways that they are done – constitutes the technology of the organization. The way in which individual members of the organization interact with other members in the course of doing things to the raw material (which may of course be other people) constitutes the organization's structure.

Perrow's view of the role of technology

Perrow distinguishes two relevant aspects of the technology of an organization that he claims are important determinants of organizational structure:

Two relevant aspects of technology

. . . the number of exceptional cases encountered in the work, that is, the degree to which stimuli are perceived as familiar or unfamiliar . . . The second is the nature of the search process that is undertaken by the individual when exceptions occur. We distinguish two types of search process. The first type involves a search which can be conducted on a logical, analytical basis . . . The second type of search process occurs when the problem is so vague and poorly conceptualized as to make it virtually unanalysable . . . In this case one draws upon the residue of unanalysable experience or intuition. (Perrow 1972a pp. 49–50.)

Using these two dimensions (each one varying between high or low, and present or absent) Perrow finds four types of technology, see Figure 1.

Perrow attaches a great deal of importance to the nature of the raw material that the organization processes. He conceives of the raw material as varying with respect to two variables: its understandability and its stability and variability. But he emphasizes that these distinctions do not refer to some actual state of the raw material, but to the

Variations in raw material processed by the organization

Figure 1 Technological variable (industrial example) Source: Perrow 1972a p. 51

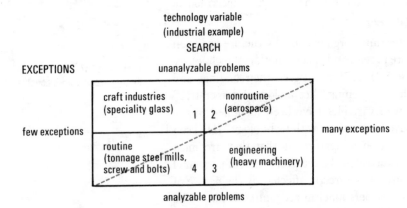

way in which it is considered and defined within the organization. He notes that organizations attempt to so define their raw material as to '. . . minimize exceptional situations.' (Perrow 1972a p. 51.) And so to open the way for rule-bound procedures and routineness.

Perrow's argument that '. . . technology is a better basis for comparing organizations than the several schemes which now exist' (Perrow 1972a p. 48) is supported by Hage and Aiken who report on the basis of their study, which attempted to explore the relationship between routine work, organizational structure and organizational goals, that Perrow's hypotheses concerning routine technology and centralized decision making were empirically substantiated. (Hage and Aiken 1972 p. 70.)

Suggested link between routine work and organizational structure confirmed by Hage and Aiken

Perrow's suggestions – and their application by Hage and Aiken – are relevant to the subject matter of these units and the previous sections not only because Perrow is concerned with modifying and refining the hypothesized significance of technology as an independent variable in analyses of organizational structure, but also because in doing so he makes some pertinent points about Woodward's conception of technology. Obviously Perrow's specific conception of technology in terms of the degree of routineness of work could be seen as broadly similar to Woodward's interest in the extent to which the '. . . production process is controllable and its results predictable'. (Woodward 1969 p. 203.) But there are also differences between the two definitions of technology. For one thing Woodward's definition is restricted to industrial applications; her three types would make little sense in organizations that process, or deal with, people. Another difficulty has been noted by Perrow who although asserting the importance of technology also notes the variety of phenomena that have been variously included in definitions of this term. Of Woodward he writes:

Differences between Perrow's work and Woodward's

> Her independent variable is not, strictly speaking, technology, but is a mixture of production, size of production run, layout of work and type of customer order. These distinctions overlap and it is difficult to decide how a particular kind of organization might be classified in her scheme or how she made her final classification. (Perrow 1972a p. 66.)

One of the points that emerges with overwhelming certainty from any review of attempts to develop organizational classification, is that, as Pugh and Hickson remark, despite the central importance of the notion of organizational structure to those who theorize about – or classify – organizations, the concept of structure '. . . remains primitive in empirical application. So far neither manager nor researcher has any means other than personal intuition of knowing how far the structure of Company A is the same as, or different from, that of Company B, or State Agency C.' (Pugh and Hicks . . . 973 p. 51.) The attempt made by these authors to develop some sort of acceptable, reliable, statistical measurement of discrete and unitary organizational characteristics has proved enormously influential. It represents a definite change in

SAQ 3 Describe and evaluate the contributions of Woodward and Perrow to the discussion of types and determinants of organizational structure

Inadequate empirical applications of concept organizational structure

strategy from those typologies which derive purely from some *a priori* theoretical or conceptual interest. This work will be considered in more detail later.

To conclude this section, which has presented a selection of organizational classifications, a number of summary remarks can be made which will serve to relate these classifications and their implicit assumptions to later sections:

1 It is generally maintained that it is important to consider the extent to which organizations, *qua* organizations, hold characteristics in common. It would seem to be a central feature of any attempt to understand a phenomenon to investigate the extent (or existence) of internal differentiation within the object of study. (Such a view is stated particularly forcibly in Blau's article 'The Comparative Study of Organizations' in Grusky and Miller.)

2 A number of different ways of classifying organizations have been put forward. Very frequently the bases of the different organizational structures that are referred to and isolated by the classification – and the mechanisms whereby these structures are produced – derive more from the theoretical perspective of the author than from any observed or measured empirical differentiation.

3 Most methods of classifying organizations have been criticized on the grounds that it is sometimes difficult to allocate organizations to one category or another, and that the basis of the classification actually fails to distinguish between or to correlate with what are usually considered to be important structural features of the organization.

4 Most organizational classifications argue that the organizational differences they claim to highlight are the result of some causal mechanism, which may be discussed either explicitly or implicitly. Frequently the causal mechanism involves reference to some state of affairs, circumstances, conditions or arrangements which are 'necessary' in order to achieve organizational goals. This issue constitutes the subject matter of the next section.

5 If the relationship between theoretically derived typologies and organizational, empirical, reality is problematic and contentious, the alternative strategy of developing empirically derived taxonomies is also of limited utility. Social reality is not simply 'out there' to be discovered and measured. Even empirical taxonomies rely upon a choice of certain variables to look for, and the difficulties of actually measuring organizational structure are considerable. Probably it is best to end with Hall's conclusion, arrived at after reviewing a number of taxonomic, typological efforts:

> Classificatory schemes are needed in every facet of social life for thought and action. Despite the need for typologies, no adequate scheme for organizations is available. The 'common-sense' divisions between profit and nonprofit or governmental and nongovernmental organizations yield more confusion than clarity. Typologies based upon a single basic principle, such as those of Parsons, Etzioni . . . do not sufficiently differentiate between organizations and do not divide organizations on more than a single meaningful issue. The attempt to derive a taxonomy from a mass of empirical data suffered because of weakness in the data and limitations on the relevance of the variables measured. (Hall 1972b p. 78.)

Summary

Importance of comparative approach and classifications of organizations

Variety of classifications

Empirical difficulties of such classifications

Determinants of organizational structure

Limited utility of empirical taxonomies

Unit 5 Organization structure: the main elements and interrelationships

5 Organizational structure, organizational goals

Although, as Child argues on the basis of his succinct summary of recent work on the determinants of organizational structure, a number of different factors have been considered as determinants of, or conditions for, such empirical variation in organizational structures as has been discovered or claimed, this section will restrict attention to the role of organizational goals in this debate.[1] This approach has been adopted because, as the discussion of organizational classifications in the previous section revealed, the concept organizational goal underlies a great deal of thinking on organizations and the claimed association between various aspects of organizational structure, or organizational environment and structure. The next section will consider some alternative ways of regarding the determinants of organizational structure, or of explaining the apparent correlations between organizational characteristics.

Organizational goals and organizational structure

It has been seen that for Parsons '. . . primacy of orientation to the attainment of a specific goal is used as the defining characteristic of an organization'. (Parsons 1970 p. 75.) This, it is claimed, has consequences for the structure and external relations of the organization. The relationship with the environment is regarded in terms of the 'maximization' of some output which supplies criteria by which the internal structure of the organization may be assessed. This has consequences for organization which Parsons sees as suffering 'deprivation' if the desired output is not achieved.

Etzioni directly addresses the importance (and nature) of organizational goals. In his scheme the theoretical possibility of nine organizational types is, it is claimed, seldom realized because three types constitute what are called *congruent* relationships between power means and orientation, and six do not. This argument has two elements. We are told that to some extent organizational power means tend to generate certain sorts of reactions (involvements) (and here lies the tautology), but that organizational members also bring involvements with them into the organization. When their prior orientations[2] are similar to the involvement they develop as a result of exposure to the organization's power the situation is described as congruent.

Etzioni and organizational goals

But it is also stated that such congruence is more efficient, and that organizations are '. . . under pressure to be effective'. (Etzioni 1970 p. 109.) Therefore, '. . . organizations tend to shift their compliance structure from incongruent to congruent types'. (Etzioni 1970 p. 108.) Since compliance structure is seen as a key variable in determining other features of the organization, and since congruence is achieved as a result of the pressure efficiently to achieve the organization's goals, it is clear that goals and goal attainment play a central part in the Etzioni model.[3]

As mentioned earlier the Woodward scheme for differentiating organizations according to what are claimed to be the observed, empirical bases of organizational, structural variation also hinges around the objectives that are being pursued. Organizational goals are held to determine the nature and organization of the manufacturing process; and this affects the structure of the organization.

Woodward and organizational goals

1 Unit 6, 'The organization as a system' also contains discussion of organizational goals, since these are central features of any attempt to conceptualize organizations in this way. A thoroughgoing critique of the systems approach (and the view of organizations as goal attaining phenomena) is contained in Silverman (1970).

2 These concepts of involvement and orientations towards work and employing organizations have been utilized by those interested in investigating the different sorts of worker attitudes and behaviour. This subject is discussed by Fox (1973).

3 Etzioni distinguishes between two sorts of functional relationship: the survival model (without this institution or feature the society or organization would not survive) and the efficiency model (this particular feature makes the system '. . . most effective in the service of a given goal'). (Etzioni 1961 p. 78.) Etzioni lists a number of intervening variables that assist the achievement of efficiency in organizations characterized by congruent compliance structures.

The authors whose schemes have been discussed here are by no means exceptional in the importance they attach to organizational goals in analyses of organization. For many sociologists, goal attainment is *the defining characteristic*. For example Blau and Scott consider that despite the obvious differences between organizations, 'What they all have in common is that a number of men have become organized into a social unit – an organization – that has been established for the explicit purpose of achieving certain goals'. (Blau and Scott 1963 p. 1.)

Similarly, it is quite orthodox to relate this attaining element to the structure of the organization, just as members are likely to do. So Mouzelis writes:

> Formal organizations are established for a certain purpose: men, in a more or less conscious way, co-ordinate their activities in order to achieve certain goals. This co-ordination necessitates a system of purposive control. It usually consists of rules which define the tasks and responsibilities of each participant as well as the formal mechanisms which could permit the integration of these tasks. Such rules constitute the formal structure of the organization. (Mouzelis 1967 p. 59.)

Because of the sociological centrality of the notion of goal in analyses, classifications and definitions of organizations, and because this concept is also used by organizational members and others in *their* understanding of the organization, it is most pertinent to consider it thoroughly and critically.[1]

One of the major difficulties with the approach is illustrated by the following quotation from a report by the Health Policy Advisory Center into the American health system, and its current crisis:

Difficulties in discovering organizational goals

> . . . the American health system is not in business for people's health . . . even within the institutions that make up America's health system – hospitals, doctors, medical schools drug companies, health insurance companies – health care does not take top priority. Health is no more a priority of the American health industry than safe, cheap, efficient pollution-free transportation is a priority of the American automobile industry. (Ehrenreich 1971 p. vi.)

In other words, from the point of view of organizational analysis the problem with the goal achievement approach to organizations is that it is by no means clear just what the goals of the organization are, and certainly the stated goals should be considered sceptically. Depending on the stance taken towards organizational goals, i.e. whether the official statements and rhetoric are accepted or viewed with cynicism, the actual behaviours and choices of senior members of the organization can be viewed with or without indignation, as extraordinarily and inexplicably deviant, or as quite natural and logical, given these 'real' goals. This initial point is made by Perrow when he argues that organizations are indeed tools, but that they are tools for many different purposes only *for those who control them*. It is thus irrelevant to criticize organizations as being inefficient because they display, for example, particular rather than universal criteria in, say, the choice and treatment of organizational personnel, because such behaviour can only be assessed as efficient or not in terms of the *actual* goals and objectives of those members who display them. '. . . organizations are tools designed to perform work for their masters, and particularism or universalism is relative to the goals of the masters.' (Perrow 1972b pp. 16–17.)[2]

It has been argued that when Weber talked of organizational rationality he

---

1 'The central concept in the study of organizations is that of organizational *goal*. One might even claim that the notion of a goal is coincident with that of an organization.' (Gross 1969 p. 277.)

2 See also Etzioni's article, 'Two Approaches to Organizational Analysis', in Grusky and Miller. In this article Etzioni expands on his distinction between an approach which measures organizations against their 'public' goals – and which results in indignation and disappointment – and an approach which focuses attention on the variety of activities and functions organization must perform and which measures efficiency relative to other organizations rather than against an ideal. Etzioni is arguing also, then, that sociologists should refrain from employing organizational 'public' goals as criteria of assessment of organizational structure or process, since these goals are not employed in this way by those working within the organization.

was referring to, or assessing, the efficiency or adequacy of some means-ends link. That is, that he was concerned with the efficiency with which organizational procedures and processes achieved the goals they were designed to achieve. Such an interpretation of Weber is now largely discredited (see Unit 1); but it is still common for those who write about organizations to attend to the relationship between what *they* take to be, or infer as, the organizational goals and organizational procedures, although this may mean rejecting one view of the organizational objectives in favour of a more realistic, or cynical one. For example, Perrow has distinguished between official goals and operative goals, the latter being seen as '. . . those that are embedded in major operating policies and the daily decisions of the personnel'. (Perrow 1961 p. 854.) These goals, Perrow continues, '. . . designate the ends sought through the actual operating policies of the organizations; they tell us what the organization actually is trying to do, regardless of what the official goals say are the aims.'[1] (Perrow 1961 p. 855.) In the same vein the Ehrenreichs argue that the American health crisis is only problematic as long as it is assumed that the health system exists to improve or look after the health of Americans, in which case its 'inefficiency' is surprising. But these authors argue that the 'health' system is oriented more towards profit-making than patient care, and that in these terms, '. . . the health industry is an extraordinarily well-organized and efficient machine'. (Ehrenreich 1971 p. 23.) Such an approach has also been used with reference to mental hospitals where the small number of trained psychiatric staff employed can belie the organizational claims to be concerned more with patient health than with custody. (See Etzioni, in Grusky and Miller for further examples.)

Varieties of organizational goals

The famous study by Michels (which is excerpted in Grusky and Miller) refers to the necessity to consider how organizations pursue goals other than those they were originally set up to achieve. In the case in point Michels considers how the fact of organization creates, through its inevitably *oligarchic* structure, groups and interests that are in conflict with the democratic basis and concerns that were the original inspiration and objective of the organization. (Michels 1970.) Michels' work also raises the likelihood that organizational goals may vary over time; that the procedures set up to achieve a state of affairs may either produce power and ability for organizational groups to pursue alternative ends, or that the means in themselves become objectives. Such a possibility serves as the starting point of David Sills' article in Grusky and Miller – 'Preserving Organizational Goals.' This article also contains some suggestions as to why goals are 'displaced' within an organization, why members are not similarly committed to the same organizational goal. (The term 'displaced', it should be noted, is somewhat unfortunate since it seems to refer to a state or period of pristine organizational innocence when organizational goals were clear and unambiguous, and all members devoted their efforts to attaining them. The whole point of this section is that goals have not been, are not, cannot be, specific guides to everyday actions and events.) Members of organizations have different goals, and different conceptions of what they take to be the organization's goals, and they have differential power and opportunities to realize or legitimate these goals. Gross has suggested the importance of distinguishing '. . . private (personal, individual) goals from organizational goals . . . what a particular person desires *for the organization as a whole*'. (Gross 1969 p. 278.) This leads to the difficulty described by Silverman: How can organizational goals be pinpointed and described? To refer back to the Ehrenreichs' analysis of the 'real' goals of the American health industry, how do these authors know what these 'real' goals are? Whose actions or words can reliably be

Changes in organizational goals

Members of organizations have different goals and different conceptions of organizational goals

How to pinpoint organizational goals

---

1 This point has also been made by Cicourel who distinguishes between the 'front' and 'back' of an organization, between official practices which '. . . are expected and accepted by others' and unofficial practices which '. . . contradict such expectations and are not viewed as "acceptable".' (Cicourel 1958 p. 54.) But this also introduces the idea of organizational goals and objectives as acceptable ways of explaining and legitimating actual behaviour rather than as determinants of it. This tack will be followed up later.

taken as genuine indicators or expressions of organizational goals? Are they the stated goals of the organization's public relations rhetoric (what Perrow would call the official goals), the goals of certain key personnel as they describe them to themselves, each other, or the researcher; the goals as they are inferred by some omniscient observer, or the requirements and constraints that members operate under in their decision making? (Silverman 1970 pp. 8–11.) Furthermore, the article by Thompson and McEwen (1973) suggests that it is important to consider organizational goals not as givens, fixed for ever, but as an aspect of an organization's functioning. They write: 'It is possible, however, to view the setting of goals (i.e. major organizational purposes) not as a static element, but as a necessary and recurring problem facing any organization.' (Thompson and McEwen 1973 p. 155.) But whatever the difficulties and problems that surround any attempt to discover what an organization's goals are, the established view is that such goals are reflected in the structure of the organization, which is seen as being designed to achieve (under pressures of efficiency or 'situational demands') the 'official' or formal goals. However the difficulty with this argument is that a lot of what goes on in organizations has nothing to do with such regulation and control and this organizational structure itself does not reflect a concern for such goals.

The sociological literature on organizations frequently contains reference to a distinction between formal and informal aspects of organizational structure. As Mouzelis and others have noted, this distinction can mean a number of different things. (Mouzelis 1967.) One common usage involves a reference to aspects of the organization's structure or process which are not defined or prescribed by the organization chart or the organizational rules, procedures and prescriptions as these are seen and described by senior organizational personnel. Such a distinction does have the benefit of drawing attention to the symbolic rather than descriptive status of such official statements of organizational structure or purpose, but it also carries dangers, as Albrow spells out in his article (1973). He notes that aspects of the organization's structure are the result of outside factors; that 'unofficial' behaviours and relationships can serve to assist the attainment of desired objectives; that the behaviour of members of organizations is not simply the result of organizational rules, regulations and constraints, and that 'the notion of the specific goal as the origin and cause of the organization is an unhistoric myth'. (Albrow 1973 p. 402.) Albrow too notes that organizational goals tend to be general, vague, multiple and confused, and asks, how then can it be argued that organizational structure (which implies some degree of orderliness and regularity) is determined by these organizational goals?[1] His solution to the difficulty is to offer an alternative definition of organizations which does not conceive of them in terms of some social contract-like consensus between the members of a co-operative group, who agree to work together in certain specific ways in order to achieve their goal. On the contrary, Albrow's view of organizations contains reference to structure or regularity between the *emergent consequence* of competition and conflict between membership groups and their various goals.[2] Such a view of organizations, and of organizational goals, is also presented by Crozier, on the

Albrow's criticism

Organizations as trends of conflict

1 This is a significant step in the argument. Up to now it has been argued that organizations tend to pursue objectives other than those they publicize and assert, and that what actually happens within the organization is not determined by a body of rules, procedures and restraints which has been designed so as to ensure or enable the achievement of the organization's goals. It is now being suggested that organizational goals are not amenable to a detailed breakdown into individual responsibilities and objectives because like any prescription, advice or rule they do not contain, intrinsically, operational blue-prints for action. It is not possible to predict the behaviours that would follow a commitment to a particular organizational goal. Now this suggestion that behavioural controls or overarching moralities should be considered not in terms of how they determine behaviour, but how they are used and referred to by those persons who are, as it were, licensed to employ them in everyday organizational life, constitutes the central theme of Block Three of this course.

2 Unit 7 deals with the interactionist perspective on organizations which focuses on the extent, importance and consequence of negotiation and exchange within organizations. Later units will also take up this theme. The article by Strauss (1973) is a classic and cogent statement of this approach.

basis of his analysis of two French bureaucracies. Although by no means denying the importance of official, formal rules and statements of goals he notes that, inevitably, organizations contain conflicts and divisions; by no means all organizational members are committed to the overall organizational goals, and the behaviour of organizational members can not realistically be viewed as attempts to attain such goals. Instead Crozier sees bureaucratization itself as an *attempt* to reduce behavioural uncertainty and eliminate unofficial power and resistance. But uncertainty survives, as do the multitude of conflicting goals and priorities, and the job of a manager, Crozier concludes, is not to pursue the clearly stated organizational goal, but to '. . . settle conflicting claims in a maze of rules, arbitrate between opposing forms of rationality, and face the difficult moral issues of the ambiguity of means and ends.' (Crozier 1964 p. 298.)

Albrow's definition raises another interesting issue in connection with this discussion of organizational goals. He sees organizations as, '. . . social units where individuals are conscious of their membership and legitimize their co-operative activities primarily by reference to the attainment of impersonal goals rather than to moral standards'. (Albrow 1973 p. 409.) Note how this raises the suggestion that organizations are phenomena which make available to their members ways and procedures for justifying (or legitimizing) and explaining their actions. Goals are now seen not as determinants of actions, but as ways of 'rationalizing' them – ways of making them sensible to those others who, as members, can be relied upon to inhabit the same symbolic and cultural community and thus to accept a particular sort of explanation, reason, complaint or suggestion as sensible and rational. Clearly this immediately introduces the possibility that different conceptions of the 'proper' organizational interest and so different organizational rationalities, may exist.

> Organizational goals as legitimating symbols

The suggestion that members' statements about goals should be seen not as determinants of behaviour or social structure, but as ways of explaining, sensibly to competent and qualified others, those behaviours which are seen as displaying ordered properties, comprises the main thrust of C. W. Mills' famous essay on 'Situated Actions and Vocabularies of Motive'. Mills' comments in this essay are relevant to the considerations of this section in as much as Mills argues for a view of motives (or goals) as '. . . typical vocabularies having ascertainable functions in delimited societal situations . . .'. (Mills 1940 p. 904.) He continues, '. . . motives are the terms with which interpretation of conduct *by social actors* proceeds. This imputation and avowal of motives by actors are social phenomena to be explained.' (Mills 1940 p. 904.) Later Mills comments that particular 'historical epochs and specified situations' (which of course include organizations) make available situational vocabularies of sensible, unquestioned, motives and answers. The goals of an organization can be seen in the same way, as organizationally available acceptable verbalizations.[1] One interesting if rather ominous implication of such a view might be that sociologists who study organizations have shown an excessive preparedness to accept what passes – within the organization, or among organizations in general – for sensible justifications and accounts; in other words in their own (sociological) accounts and descriptions they have relied upon organizational members' descriptions and explanations.

> Organizations as supplying vocabularies of motives

Finally, Selznick's study of the Tennessee Valley Authority in America is also pertinent to this discussion. Selznick notes how this particular organization attempted to disseminate statements of its intentions and goals – he writes of the leaders of the TVA that they '. . . have been especially active . . . in propagating a systematic formulation of its own meaning and significance'. (Selznick 1966 p. 21.) But Selznick

> Selznick's study of the TVA

---

1 Such an argument can – and later will – lead to a consideration of other elements of sociological theorizing about organizations in terms of their reliance upon, and utilization in terms of, everyday inmate or member thinking, accounting and talking about the organization. Amongst a number of relevant articles in Salaman and Thompson (1973) the most pertinent at this stage is Bittner's 'The Concept of Organization'.

goes on to show how these goals, although indisputably important as overall symbols, were not in fact always realized in action. The notion of grass-roots administration was a key element in the organizational rhetoric. But Selznick notes that the '. . . needs of maintaining the organization tend to drive it toward alliances and mechanisms of participation . . .' which are at odds with the spirit of the rather vaguely phrased commitments to '. . . the exercise of democracy'. (Selznick 1966 p. 60.) A number of points emerge: first that goals tend to be so vague and general as to be inadequate as guides to action although important symbolically. Secondly, that the actual behaviour of members of organizations is determined more by the conflict between opposing factional interests within the organization or between it and the environment, than by any overarching organizational goal.

Goals too vague to act as guides to action

Official organizational goals do not determine members' actions

To summarize this section:

1 For many who work in, are dealt with, treated or processed by, or who study organizations, the concept of organizational goal typically figures as a central, explanatory variable. Criticisms, descriptions and definitions are frequently couched in terms of what the organization is trying to do. For this reason the concept has been exposed to a certain rather critical scrutiny in these units; particularly since the classifications mentioned earlier tend to orientate around a view of organizations as goal-attaining phenomena.

Importance of concept organizational goal to some who study or work in organizations

2 The idea that the structure of the organization – the way things are meant to be done, by whom, when and how – is designed to achieve the goals of the organization (a view that is held quite explicitly by some sociologists who have studied organizations) has been criticized. Of course, it is true, as Silverman notes, that organizations may be '. . . consciously established to serve certain purposes which are generally stated at the time'. And that 'their founder(s) further provide them with a set of rules which generally lay down clear lines of authority and communication with the intention of ensuring that these purposes may be most readily attained'. (Silverman 1970 p. 14.) The point is though that such goals will not be shared by all members of the organization; that the intended connection between formal structure (which is anyway problematically related to actual events and behaviour) and the goals is probably unsuccessful; that such goals themselves are too vague to act as guides to action; and that members of ongoing organizations develop their own priorities and goals.

Organizational structure not simply designed to achieve organizational goals

The stated goals are more significant for their symbolic, legitimating function than for their determination of actual courses of action, it has been claimed, and members of organizations tend to behave in 'informal' ways to pursue what they take to be their own desired ends. Organizations can be seen not as scientifically designed systems created to attain some overarching objective, but as congeries of interests and conflicts among groups with differing amounts of power and influence pursuing their own goals and objectives. Organizational structure can thus be seen as an attempt, on the part of one organizational group, to so control other members as to stop them from having any capacity to achieve their own divergent goals. For this reason, formal organizational rules, procedures, prescriptions, etc. will be resisted and avoided when possible.

3 But despite all this organizations can be seen – indeed are seen – as oriented towards certain goals, by those who work in or for them. The distinctive feature of organizational life is the vocabulary of acceptable motives and justifications that are made available to members. In organizations as against other social collectivities the available culture of symbols and legitimations contains reference to notions of rationality. This notable feature of organizations was of course considered in Unit 1, where it was mentioned that Weber's early sociological interest in organizations focused directly on the question of authority – that is the conditions and circumstances under which persons accepted and justified their subordination to power. Bureaucracy, Weber stressed, represented, in a highly developed form,

Organizational goals as legitimating symbols

a particular type of (rational-legal) authority. It is possible to see the relationship between this interest of Weber's and the general line of the argument of this section: organization can be seen in terms of the ways in which they depend upon and make available legitimating symbols, ideas and definitions, among which are the goals of the organizations. Once these have been accepted the question of actual organizational behaviour in the world becomes restricted to evaluations of the rationality or technical efficiency of the activities of members of the organization with reference to these stated goals.

The behaviour of organizational members, far from consensually following some solidaristic commitment to all overall organizational goals (or the organizational structure which somehow emerges from this goal) actually follows from their attempts to pursue their own priorities and interests within the contraints surrounding their location within the organizational structure, and the resulting behaviour is explained and justified (or permitted) by reference to the goals of the organization.

4 These units started with some discussion and justification of the structural perspective on organizations. Attempts to classify or measure organizational structure

SAQ 4 In what way have organizations been seen in terms of their goals? What are the inadequacies of regarding organizations in this way?

Figure 2 Industrial society: a Swiss cartoon

Source: Nebelspalter 1970 (drawn by Hans-Georg Rauch and used by permission of the artist)

have encountered a variety of difficulties. The goal-attaining model has been shown to be particularly suspect. But if variations in organizational structure do exist and can be measured or observed, then what determines these differences? This will constitute the subject matter of the next section.

SAQ 5 What are the goals of your employing organization? How do you know? Whose goals are these? Do they differ from the official goals? To what extent, if at all, do such goals affect the structure of the organization?

6 The determinants of organizational structure: the role of choice

Blau and Schoenherr, who are two notable representatives of the structuralist approach to organizations, explain and justify their approach in terms of the 'regularities' that organizations exhibit which may be 'analysed in their own right, independent of any knowledge about the individual behaviour of their members'. (Blau and Schoenherr 1971 p. viii.) It has been seen that analyses of these regularities frequently tend to be based either upon pre-existing theoretical commitments or upon the analyses, definitions and descriptions of senior members of the organization, and their 'knowledge' or view of the organization and its symbolic, cultural equipment.

However it is one thing to point out the difficulties that are often encountered in using a concept, or an approach, and another to reject the concept altogether. Few would deny that organizations do exhibit regularities of one sort or another; although some would maintain that such regularity and orderliness as is displayed and made apparent is not the result of organizational members' obeying official rules and regulations, but of a series of ongoing negotiations and compromises between conflicting and competing groups whose power in these negotiations derives from internal and external factors. Position within the organization and control over various organizational activities (among which would be the capacity or prerogative to design and enforce organizational procedures) constitutes an important source of organizational power. In these interest conflicts the goals of the organization and other symbols will be mobilized for legitimating purposes.

Organizational regularity

Organizational structure emerges out of relations between organizational groups and members

Such a conception of organizational structure does not deny that organizations reveal, or create regularities, it merely emphasizes that these are the consequences of the combinations and interactions of various individual or group priorities, aspirations and constraints. Man *need not* be left out of discussions of structure.

The discussion of a selection of organizational classifications, however, revealed another way in which man had been left out. This omission concerns the mechanisms whereby the claimed relationship between the selected key variable (goals, compliance structure, technology) obtained. Frequently, as noted, this imputed mechanism involved some reference to the goals of the organization and their achievement. This sort of suggestion has been critically considered, but the question of the nature of the processes that produce the correlations between elements within organizational structure, or between other variables and the organization's structure, remains.

How is claimed relationship between structure and selected variable achieved?

Here, as elsewhere, there has been a tendency to leave men out, to consider the relationship between, say, technology or environment and the structure of the organization in a mechanical way as the outcome of some 'necessary', or functionally imperative process. As Child (1973) points out, however, this argument is inadequate because '. . . it fails to give due attention to the agency of choice by whoever have the power to direct the organization'. (Child 1973 p. 91.) The regularities that lie behind discussions of organizational structure consist of the behaviour of men; men do not normally consider a 'functional imperative', system need or 'situational demand' when choosing and planning their own behaviours. Consequently any *explanation* (rather than merely description of an observed correlation) must at some stage contain reference to men's choices and considerations.

Mechanistic conceptions of determinants of organizational structure

Child's insistence on role of choice in construction of organizational structure

How then does the claimed relationship between, for example, compliance structure and organizational structure or technology and structure come about? Presumably unless it occurs through some process whereby organizations that do not display the correlation go out of existence, or unless the classification is entirely axiomatic, the relationship between the key variable and organizational structure must rest upon decisions taken by those persons responsible for and able to control and design the structure of the organization in terms of what could be taken to be their 'rationality', that is *their* grasp or conception of the relationship between the organizational goals as they see them and the optimum organizational structure or design. Recent work has argued this case strongly, that organizational structure is not the consequence of some inexorable organizational logic, but a result of the values, aspirations and notions of what a proper organization looks like that are held by those members of the organization with the power to control and initiate structure. Thus organizational structure, which as later units will point out, consists of restriction on and control over members' decision making, is itself the outcome of power struggles between politically salient groups within the organization. (With the help, prescriptions and principles of organizational ideologues and theoreticians such as the 'classical management thinkers'.)[1]

Child's article considers a number of orthodox models of the determinants or correlates of organizational structure and argues convincingly that all involve a considerable element of choice. For example, with respect to technology he suggests that, 'The prevailing technology is now seen as a *product* of decisions on workplans, resources and equipment which were made in the light of certain evaluations of the organization's positions in its environment'. (Child 1972 p. 6. My emphasis.)[2]

Child argues then, on the basis of his review of the three most significant and appealing models of structural determination that decisions and choices made by '. . . those who have the power of structural initiation – the dominant coalition' (Child 1973 p. 105) are important causes of variation in organizational structure. Such decisions and choices must of course be made within a framework of organizational activity, structure and environment which is constraining, but these factors themselves involve choices, as well as leaving considerable room for manoeuvre.

Argyris too considers that the sorts of correlations between aspects of organizational structure reported by Blau do not reflect any general organizational laws, but the values and conceptions of those with the capacity to initiate structure. His article is also interesting for the comments it contains on the difficulties of measuring or describing organizational structure.

The concept structure, when it is applied to organizations, refers to the extent to which and the ways in which organizations' members are constrained and controlled by the organization and distribution of activities and responsibilities and the organizational procedures and regulations. Not surprisingly therefore, types and procedures of· organizational control have always been a central concern of those sociologists who theorize about or study organizations, and organizational structure. Interest in organizational control has of course an added salience because of Weber's suggestion that bureaucratic organization represents in an extreme form a particular type of authority.

Earlier sections distinguished between theoretically derived typologies and empirically grounded taxonomies (although this distinction should be seen as involving a quantitative rather than qualitative difference). Both sorts of classification have been concerned with theorizing about or investigating processes and types of organizational control (see Etzioni for example). The next section will consider some of this

---

1 Outside factors are important too, obviously. Structure can be significantly affected by government regulations, training board requirements and so on. It is also affected by the extra-organizational values, attitudes and commitment of the organizational members, as Albrow argues.

2 It is possible to see some degree of awareness of this possibility in the writings of those who argue for the determinate importance of technology. As noted, Perrow suggests the nature of the raw material is important, but he adds, 'We are not referring here to the "essence" of the material, only to the way the organization itself perceives it.' (Perrow 1972a p. 50.) Similarly Woodward writes: 'Organizations appeared to grow in response to a number of stimuli. The "organization conscious" firms tended to draw on the concepts of management theory, irrespective of how appropriate they were to the technical situation. Fashion was another important factor.' (Woodward 1969 p. 228.) Interestingly she later refers to this event as a 'distortion'. The point raised by Child and Argyris is that the 'technical situation' itself involves choices and decisions.

Organizational structure a result of values of those concerned

Determinate role of technology questioned

work on what are claimed to be variations in organizational structure with special reference to processes of organizational control.

7 Differences in organizational structures: types of organizational control

Max Weber's delineation of the bureaucratic ideal type has served as the inspiration of a great deal of work into organizational control mechanisms and types. The characteristics Weber regarded as bureaucratic – the existence and application of rules, hierarchic offices, emphasis on technical competence and so on – constitute a particular sort of organizational control, but *possibly not the only one*.

Organizational control

Two points of interest each deriving from Weber's writings lie behind a great deal of work discussed below. A number of writers have concerned themselves with establishing the empirical interrelationships between the characteristics that Weber considered to be distinctively bureaucratic. Such work argues that bureaucracy – in terms of Weber's dimensions – can be seen not as '. . . a condition that is either present or absent . . .' but as '. . . a form of organization which exists along a number of continua or dimensions'. (Hall 1963 p. 33.)[1]

Relationships between Weber's bureaucratic features

The empirical interrelationships between Weberian bureaucratic dimensions have also been investigated by Udy. However his work has added significance for this discussion since he argues that Weber himself implicitly distinguished between two types of bureaucracy and that these suggested clusterings of interrelated variables are empirically apparent. More specifically Udy suggests that Weber distinguished between bureaucratic elements ('. . . hierarchic authority structure, an administrative staff, and differential rewards according to office'), and rational elements ('Limited objectives, a performance emphasis, segmental participation and compensatory rewards'). (Udy 1959 p. 793.) Udy claims that 'Bureaucracy and rationality tend to be mutually inconsistent in the same formal organization'. (Udy 1969 p. 794.)

Udy distinguishes two types of bureaucracy

The suggestion that bureaucratic administration and control can be distinguished empirically from other sorts of (rational) organization and control constitutes the central argument of Stinchcombe's article 'Bureaucratic and Craft Administration' in Grusky and Miller. The two forms of organization isolated by Stinchcombe differ in the ways in which members are controlled – in one case by training and socialization into the ' . . . empirical lore that makes up craft principles', in the other by '. . . centralized planning of work'. (Stinchcombe 1970 pp. 262 and 263.)

Stinchcombe's types

Stinchcombe's work is interesting not only because it suggests that the Weberian bureaucratic dimensions tend to interrelate in a greater variety of ways than has been considered by those who regarded bureaucracy as an empirical realization of the Weberian ideal type, but also because it introduces a much discussed distinction between types of organizational control. This distinction, which has been variously defined and named, also stems from Parsons' famous footnoted comment which argued that Weber's view of bureaucracy involved two sources of authority, one based on technical expertise, and the other on bureaucratic position, on sheer incumbency of office. As noted earlier, this distinction has been taken up and elaborated by Gouldner, most notably in his classic *Patterns of Industrial Bureaucracy*. Gouldner distinguishes between two types of bureaucracy, one where authority is based on technical expertise and knowledge, and where there is a considerable degree of low level involvement in decisions and commitment to what are seen to be sensible and mutually agreed rules and procedures, and the other where procedures, rules and decisions are highly centralized and enforced through discipline.

Types of control in organizations

---

1   Hall develops a list of six dimensions (derived primarily from Weber). His research leads him to argue that these dimensions are not necessarily highly interrelated: that organizations that are high on one dimension are *not necessarily* high on any other. He concludes, '. . . in the organizations studied, the bureaucratic dimensions existed independently in the form of continua'. (Hall 1963 p. 39.)

This distinction between organizational control of a bureaucratic sort, exercised through centralized, rule-bound procedures and decisions, and organizational control through delegated decision making based upon occupational professional standards, techniques and knowledge (with all the concomitant implications for the 'shape' of the organization) found early exposition in the work of Burns and Stalker, and obviously relates to the two types of organizational authority described by Gouldner and mentioned earlier. These authors argued that the bureaucratic type (which they call mechanistic) consists of specialized differentiation of work duties and tasks, very specific delineation of areas of activity, responsibility and authority and a hierarchic control structure. The organic type of organizational control is characterized by constantly changing definitions of members' jobs and a greater emphasis on technical knowledge and expertise – as it is distributed throughout the organization. Because of the frequency with which the sort of distinction proposed by Burns and Stalker has been referred to and discussed, it is worthwhile to present it in full. However, the suggested distinction will be treated somewhat sceptically in these units and others in the course.

Burns and Stalker's classification of types of organizational control

---

A *mechanistic* management system is appropriate to stable conditions. It is characterized by:

a the specialized differentiation of functional tasks into which the problems and tasks facing the concern as a whole are broken down;

b the abstract nature of each individual task, which is pursued with techniques and purposes more or less distinct from those of the concern as a whole, i.e. the functionaries tend to pursue the technical improvement of means, rather than the accomplishment of the ends of the concern;

c the reconciliation, for each level in the hierarchy, of these distinct performances by the immediate superiors, who are also, in turn, responsible for seeing that each is relevant in his own special part of the main task;

d the precise definition of rights and obligations and technical methods attached to each functional role;

e the translation of rights and obligations and methods into the responsibilities of a functional position;

f hierarchic structure of control, authority and communication;

g a reinforcement of the hierarchic structure by the location of knowledge of actualities exclusively at the top of the hierarchy, where the final reconciliation of distinct tasks and assessment of relevance is made;

h a tendency for interaction between members of the concern to be vertical, i.e. between superior and subordinate;

i a tendency for operations and working behaviour to be governed by the instructions and decisions issued by superiors;

j insistence on loyalty to the concern and obedience to superiors as a condition of membership;

k a greater importance and prestige attaching to internal (local) than to general (cosmopolitan) knowledge, experience, and skill.

The *organic* form is appropriate to changing conditions, which give rise constantly to fresh problems and unforeseen requirements for action which cannot be broken down or distributed automatically arising from the functional roles defined within a hierarchic structure. It is characterized by:

a the contributive nature of special knowledge and experience to the common task of the concern;

b the 'realistic' nature of the individual task, which is seen as set by the total situation of the concern;

c the adjustment and continual re-definition of individual tasks through interaction with others;

d the sheddding of 'responsibility' as a limited field of rights, obligations and methods. (Problems may not be posted upwards, downwards or sideways as being someone else's responsibility);

e the spread of commitment to the concern beyond any technical definition;

f a network structure of control, authority and communication. The sanctions which apply to the individual's conduct in his working role derive more from presumed community of interest with the rest of the working organization in the survival and growth of the firm, and less from a contractual relationship between himself and a non-personal corporation, represented for him by an immediate superior;

g omniscience no longer imputed to the head of the concern; knowledge about the technical or commercial nature of the here and now task may be located anywhere in the network; this location becoming the *ad hoc* centre of control authority and communication;

h a lateral rather than a vertical direction of communication through the organization, communication between people of different rank, also, resembling consultation rather than command;

i a content of communication which consists of information and advice rather than instructions and decisions;

j commitment to the concern's tasks and to the 'technological ethos' of material progress and expansion is more highly valued than loyalty and obedience;

k importance and prestige attach to affiliations and expertise valid in the industrial and technical and commercial milieux external to the firm.

One important corollary to be attached to this account is that while organic systems are not hierarchic in the same sense as are mechanistic, they remain stratified. Positions are differentiated according to seniority, i.e. greater expertise. The lead in joint decisions is frequently taken by seniors, but it is an essential presumption of the organic system that the lead, i.e. 'authority', is taken by whoever shows himself most informed and capable, i.e. the 'best authority'. The location of authority is settled by consensus.

A second observation is that the area of commitment to the concern – the extent to which the individual yields himself as a resource to be used by the working organization – is far more extensive in organic than in mechanistic systems. Commitment, in fact, is expected to approach that of the professional scientist to his work, and frequently does. One further consequence of this is that it becomes far less feasible to distinguish 'informal' from 'formal' organization.

Thirdly, the emptying out of significance from the hierarchic command system, by which co-operation is ensured and which serves to monitor the working organization under a mechanistic system, is countered by the development of shared beliefs about the values and goals of the concern. The growth and accretion of institutionalized values, beliefs, and conduct, in the form of commitments, ideology, and manners, around an image of the concern in its industrial and commercial setting make good the loss of formal structure.

Finally, the two forms of system represent a polarity, not a dichotomy; there are, as we have tried to show, intermediate stages between the extremities empirically known to us. Also, the relation of one form to the other is elastic, so that a concern oscillating between relative stability and relative change may also oscillate between the two forms. A concern may (and frequently does) operate with a management system which includes both types. (Burns and Stalker 1961 pp. 119–22.)

Interestingly Burns and Stalker, like Stinchcombe, maintain that these different types of organization are appropriate to, or efficient in, different conditions and circumstances. The key environmental variable in both cases is stability. Stinchcombe argues, for example, that '. . . professionalization of manual labour is more efficient in construction because bureaucratic administration is dependent on stability of work flow and income, and the construction industry is economically unstable'. (Stinchcombe 1970 p. 262.)[1] Burns and Stalker argue that the mechanistic organizational form is most suitable for stable environmental conditions, while the organic variant

Determinants of organizational types

---

[1] It will be seen how this argument fits in with Perrow's suggestions for the determinate significance of the routineness of the technology.

is 'appropriate to changing conditions, which give rise constantly to fresh problems and unforeseen requirements for action which cannot be broken down or distributed automatically arising from the functional roles defined within a hierarchic structure'. (Burns and Stalker 1961 p. 120.)

The suggestion that organizations tend to use two functionally equivalent types of control mechanisms has been very frequently made. Usually the argument is that while one type relies '. . . upon the skills and expertise of its members . . . the centralized arrangement relies upon rules. The former appears to emphasize self-control while the latter appears to emphasize close supervision as a mechanism of control'. (Hage and Aiken 1967 p. 90.) Furthermore as mentioned above, it is usually maintained that this difference in type of control is related to the organization's technologies, markets, environments and so on.

Two equivalent control mechanisms in organizations

This claimed difference in organizational structures relates clearly to what is often held to be the defining feature of professional groups – namely their reliance upon self control (backed up in the last resort only by sanctions) deriving from commitment to a shared body of knowledge and values and from membership of a personally significant colleague group. Such control emphasizes (and evaluates) the necessity of individual practitioners making professional decisions with reference to the shared knowledge of the profession. Control through procedures, rules and regulations created elsewhere would usually be seen as directly antithetical to the professional control system.

Distinction related to professional control mechanisms

This issue is addressed by Hall in his article 'Professionalization and Bureaucratization' (1973). Hall considers, on the basis of the research reported in this article that although the gross polarization of bureaucratic and professional forms of control is overstated, '. . . a generally inverse relationship exists between the levels of bureaucratization and professionalization. Autonomy, as an important professional attribute, is most strongly inversely related to bureaucratization'. (Hall 1973 p. 132.) Hall goes on to add that this conflict can however be overemphasized, and that the structure (that is the degree of bureaucratization) of an organization is affected by the demands and expectations – and bargaining power, presumably – of the professionals who enter the organization. In considering organizational structure as a result of compromise and conflict between various organizational groups, Hall is employing a conception of organizational structure that is more fully discussed in Strauss' article (1973). The idea that organizations rely on and employ different types of control mechanisms, and that these essentially differ with respect to the degree of rule-boundness that exists (as against reliance on individual discretion and judgement) has been put forward numerous times in various shapes and guises, as David Hickson's article 'A Convergence in Organization Theory' shows.

Hall's article

Organizational structure affected by professionals' demands

The usual argument about organic, professional type organizational control is that members of such organizations are controlled not through their exposure to organizational rules and procedures, but by their commitment to an expert or professional body of values and knowledge (this is why it is usually claimed professionals are unhappy and frustrated in 'bureaucratic' organizations). Members of organizations characterized by what Hickson (1973) has called 'lower specificity' organizational roles are seen then as making their decisions and choices in terms of their expert/professional competences and knowledge, rather than organizational rules and procedures. It would be expected then that low specificity organizations – where individual members are, relatively, free from organizational control of a direct sort – would be decentralized organizations, where these *relatively* autonomous organizational members can be free to employ their expert or professional judgement in making quite far-reaching organizational decisions. Equally, it might seem likely that organizations that involved a clear, tight and specific control of work roles and responsibilities would be highly centralized in terms of decision making. However, it will be seen that this generalization depends on what is meant by decentralization.

Professional control

Suggested relationship between centralization and formalization

The important distinction to emphasize is between a real devolution of power (which may occur with professionals who can obtain some degree of discretionary autonomy because of their powerful bargaining position) and the sort of apparent delegation of decision making responsibility where it is found that any delegation is hedged around with rules and procedures. This is the sort of situation described by Blau and Schoenherr.

The established way of conceptualizing and operationalizing the suggested variation in organizational control processes is to consider the relationship between what is called formalization (which refers to the existence and use of rules within the organization) and centralization (which refers to where decisions are taken within the organization).

It has already been pointed out that the various features of a Weberian, ideal type bureaucracy do not always co-exist, and this is also true of the suggested co-existence of formalization and centralization. These bureaucratic dimensions vary independently, indeed to some extent they are inversely related. This suggests that each characteristic represents a distinct type of organizational control, and that organizational members may be controlled *in one of two ways*: they can be constrained through their subjection to a large body of defined rules, regulations and procedures (high formalization) or they can be constrained by the fact that all the significant decisions are made at the top of the organization (highly centralized). It has often been found that when there is a high degree of formalization – clearly defined and rigidly obeyed rules and procedures – then power is delegated within organizations. Blau for example, maintains that 'Formalized procedures and centralized authority may not be two expressions of the same underlying emphasis on strict discipline, but they may rather be two alternative mechanisms for limiting the arbitrary exercise of discretion'. (Blau 1970b p. 152.) When organizational personnel can be relied upon to conform with certain general organizational priorities and procedures they may be allowed to 'exercise their own discretion' and make the appropriate decisions themselves. It may of course be asked with Argyris whether such 'decentralized' decision making can genuinely be considered as evidence of decentralization – since what seems to be occurring is that '. . . managerial decisions in organizations are either significant, in which case they are not delegated, or delegated, in which case they are not significant.' (Blau 1970b p. 172.)

There is considerable support for the argument that organizations control their members either directly, through centralized decision making, or through ensuring their obedience with or conformity to such procedures and systems that an appearance of decentralization can be achieved without any real risk of 'irresponsible' behaviour. As mentioned, Blau and Schoenherr's work argues this position strongly. It is also one of the findings of Pugh and Hickson's study (1973). These authors noticed that their empirical investigations suggested the existence of certain clusterings of interrelated organizational characteristics. Two such types that they discern which are relevant to this discussion are differentiated in terms of the sort of structuring they involve. The *workflow structured* organizations, which are relatively decentralized, '. . . have gone a long way in *structuring* activities; that is, the intended behaviour of employees has been structured by the specification of their specialized roles, of the procedures they are to follow in carrying out these roles, and of the documentation involved in what they have to do.' (Pugh and Hickson 1973 p. 62.)[1]

But another organizational type these authors delineate involves a positive relationship between centralized authority and the existence of procedures and regulations. This relationship exists only with reference to the recruitment and selection of

Two types of organizational control: high formalization and high centralization

Elimination of genuine freedom, allied to an appearance of decentralization

Pugh and Hickson's distinction between workflow and employment structures related to the two control types

[1] Later on these authors make exactly the point being argued here, when they say, '. . . authority can safely be decentralized because the organizational machine will smoothly run, as it has been set to run'. (Pugh and Hickson 1973 p. 62.)

organizational personnel. Organizations which exerted strong central control over these activities are called *employment structured*. They tend to leave actual daily work activities relatively ill-defined, possibly because control here is exercised through the '. . . central control of recruitment, central interviewing by formally constituted selection boards', and so on. (Pugh and Hickson 1973 p. 62.) As noted, Blau and Schoenherr argue most forcibly for the significance of what they consider to be a discernible shift in emphasis from control through centralized decision making to control through selection, recruitment and allocation of personnel and through the allocation of personnel resources. This new form of what they term 'insidious control' enables senior members of the organization to delegate decision making (which they are forced to do through the pressure of large volumes of complex activities and responsibilities) to middle managers, confident in their ultimate capacity to control and influence the resultant decisions by establishing the parameters of the decision making, ensuring that the personnel involved are 'properly' trained, motivated and informed, and so on.

Blau and Schoenherr argue that a change in control mechanisms is discernible

Clearly investigation of the degree of centralization within organizations is going to be a problematic exercise since it is now being argued that merely to discover where decisions within the organization are typically taken is inadequate since the most significant form of power within organizations or elsewhere is the ability *to establish the premises upon which organizational decisions are taken*. Two readings in Salaman and Thompson (1973) (Perrow, and Blau and Schoenherr) consider this point. The important thing to remember is that there are numerous ways in which the decisions and choices of members of organizations can be influenced and constrained. Two obvious examples are assembly line work and automation. But more subtle examples are apparent: for example statistical performance records, as Blau reports (1963), or standardized selection procedures or the sort of mechanisms reported in the piece by Perrow.

Need to establish not where organizational decisions are taken, but whether or not the decision maker is controlled in any way

It could be useful then to realize that various sorts of decisions are taken within organizations. The most apparent may be the least important. In his analysis of the relationship between workers' expectations of their employment situations and the nature of such situations (and how this affects workers' notions of legitimacy) Fox suggests a distinction between substantive and procedural norms. Procedural norms are those which lie behind and govern '. . . the decision making methods by which norms are formulated'. (Fox 1973 p. 322.) Substantive norms '. . . emanating from these decision making procedures, cover every aspect of organizations' activities'. (Fox 1973 p. 322.) Fox notes what this means: '. . . decisions constantly have to be taken, explicitly or implicitly, about which norms are to be used in dealing with a particular situation, problem, or instance'. (Fox 1973 p. 322.) It will be seen that this has an obvious application to the discussion of types of organizational control over decision making. It has been argued above that organizational members may appear to be free to make decisions according to their judgements and evaluations, but that such freedom may be more apparent than real, because they may be so hedged around with insidious controls which limit the available resources and options, so limited by the organizational definition of the nature of the problem, so well trained, motivated, selected, appraised, evaluated and generally processed, that when it comes to making a decision they fully conform with higher levels' priorities and expectations. They are reliable, even though they are relatively free from centralized control. In other words the decisions they make are about procedural rather than substantive matters.

Fox distinguishes between types of norms: the distinction applied to decisions

Decision making autonomy more apparent than real?

Using the same distinction Hage and Aiken have argued that professional alienation and unhappiness are related to the degree of centralization and formalization of the organization. Interestingly, these authors also distinguish between two elements of centralization that parallel Fox's distinction. They say:

Hage and Aiken: how centralization involves two elements

> Organizations vary in the extent to which members are assigned tasks and then provided with the freedom to implement them without interruption from superiors. . . . A second,

and equally important, aspect of the distribution of power is the degree to which staff members participate in setting the goals and policies of the entire organization. (Aiken and Hage 1970 p. 518.)[1]

The question remains however: if organizations with large numbers of professional and expert staff tend to display somewhat different structures, and if professionals and experts (of whom there are ever increasing numbers in organizations) are oriented towards and committed to their professional body of knowledge and colleague control – rather than organizational control, then does this mean that professional/ expert members of organizations are less controlled by the organization, that they are to some extent free to pursue their own (professional) objectives rather than the organization's? It is difficult to answer this question because, as has been argued, the structure of an organization can be seen as a result of the interactions, compromises and conflicts of competing groups within the organization – and their expectations, ideologies and definitions. In this process professionals, as Hall shows, have some possibility of influencing organizational structure and activities. But at the same time there is little, if any, evidence that organizations which employ professionals behave in a markedly different way from other organizations. Indeed it would seem that professionals – despite their agonized protestations of alienation and frustration – conform, on the whole, to their organizationally determined tasks, objectives and procedures. This leads to the possibility that professional knowledge, training and commitment are by no means necessarily antipathetic to organizational activities and objectives, except with respect to the actual organization of the work situation, and that professionals are in a rather similar situation to those other members of organizations, described by Blau and Schoenherr and others, who are free to act autonomously as long as their decisions are appropriate and conform to organization notions of rationality. However, the question of the interrelationship between bureaucracy and professionals probably depends on the type of professional, and especially the strength of the professional ideology, commitment to it, and to the professional association, and the importance or centrality of the professional's contribution. Doctors and academics probably have greater influence than research experts in a 'line' function in a commercial company.

Similarly, professionals in organizations can be seen as simply applying their expert knowledge and skills to the resolution of problems set by the organization. As Perrow has remarked, it is still the organization that defines the problem and sets the standards. And certainly it is the organization that has final control through the manipulation of resources. It is best to leave the last word on this discussion of suggested varieties of organizational control structures to Perrow: 'If we should fear large, bureaucratic organizations . . . we will not be saved from their selfish ravages by believing that they are disappearing, to be replaced by highly decentralized, problem-solving, profession-loaded organizations concerned with a responsible approach to society's multiplying social problems.' (Perrow 1972b p. 175.)[2]

Are professionals less controlled than other members of the organization?

Professionals have some say in determining organization structure

Professionals seen to conform to organizational control

Organizations set limits and premises to professional decision making

SAQ 6 To what extent do organizations display different control structures?

1 It is true then that to the extent that professionals are exposed to bureaucratic controls and regulations they tend to display unhappiness and to make such questionnaire responses as can easily be classified as displaying (or being symptomatic of) alienation. But Perrow has warned that such responses should be approached with a certain degree of cynicism. And Cotgrove and Box have shown that professionals (like everyone else) tend to manage a greater degree of compromise than might be expected. (Perrow 1972b and Cotgrove and Box 1970.)

2 Confirming evidence of this argument is supplied by the examples of universities, or health organizations. It has been argued most cogently that some American universities have tended to expend much more effort on business problems of one sort or another, or on raising government grants to finance 'practical' research than on social problems or teaching students. Indeed in some cases American universities have directly caused social problems. A similar argument can be made and has been made about the American health system which is increasingly dominated by enormous health empires, and, it is claimed, decreasingly concerned with local or national health, preventive medicine or patient care.

8 Summary

Units 4 and 5 have covered a wide range of issues and a great deal of material. But a number of points can be listed which have constituted the central themes.

1 A view of organizations as displaying ordered, regular properties and events characterizes a great deal of sociological and lay thinking on organizations. Attempts to consider and describe the structure of organizations – or to explain why and how different structures are apparent – have typically relied upon some sort of classificatory scheme. Some of these schemes have been critically discussed. *(Notion of structure basic to sociology)*

2 Two difficulties were isolated: in some cases the typologies derived elegantly from a particular theoretical perspective, or revealed a nice conceptual neatness, but were tenuously related to what other sociologists claimed were real, empirical findings and variations. At the same time more empirical taxonomies experienced difficulties in choosing the relevant variables and in measuring them. A major difficulty in empirical descriptions of organizational structure was that structure has a symbolic, normative significance as well as an empirical existence. These two tend to be confused. *(Theoretical and empirical typologies)*

3 The notion of organizational structure lies behind a great deal of thinking and theorizing about organizations. It has been held that the structure of an organization is affected by, or is designed to achieve, the goals of the organization. Some difficulties that attend this suggestion were mentioned. *(Idea that organizational structure is designed to achieve organizational goals is questioned)*

4 Despite the difficulties in describing organizational structure it was felt that a commitment to the idea that organizations did involve some sort of temporal regularity was useful and necessary, but this should be considered as a result of the conflicts, compromises and negotiations of members of the organization. At the same time the edicts, resolutions, intentions and actions of senior members of the organization with respect to the 'design' of the organization, its technology, organization of work and so on was a very major element. It was pointed out that the role of senior organizational members' choices and decisions in influencing organizational structure had been seriously underestimated. *(Organizational structure an emergent feature)*

5 Organizational structure also refers to processes and procedures of organizational control. Some research into different organizational control mechanisms was discussed – namely the low versus high role specificity types. On the basis of recent work on the relationship between formalization and centralization it was suggested that organizations tend to control members' behaviour and decision making in two different ways: through centralized decision making, or through delegation in a context where the decisions to be made consisted of purely technical matters. It was also argued that despite impressions to the contrary there was no evidence that professionals and experts in organizations were not subject to a very similar sort of control. Certainly the actions of organizations with large numbers of professional staff do not support the argument that professionals within organizations will be especially concerned with extra-organizational issues and priorities – of an occupational or societal sort. *(Different forms of organizational control considered: little evidence that either involved much discretion)*

Answers to self-assessment questions

Answer SAQ 1

a The Parsonian scheme involves the application of his general theoretical framework to organizations.

b This involves considering organizations as systems with four basic systemic problems: adaptation; goal achievement; integration and latency.

c Organizational systems, like social systems, involve subsidiary sub-systems.

d Using the four system problems Parsons distinguishes four types of organization with reference to organizational goals or functions.

e Parsons considers organizations in terms of their societal mandate to execute societally important activities.

f This conception of organizations as inevitably legitimate was questioned.

g The fact that organizations may *create* their own legitimacy seems to have been overlooked.

h The reliance of the Parsonian scheme on organizational goals was criticized.

i The utility of Parsons' scheme for actually distinguishing organizations was also questioned.

Answer SAQ 2

a Etzioni's classification and conceptualization of organizations is based upon two variables – one structural (power means) and one motivational (orientations).

b Combining these two variables results in compliance.

c Because Etzioni maintains there are three types of power and three types of orientation his scheme necessarily results in the theoretical possibility of nine compliance structures.

d However, in practice only three types are frequently found.

e Etzioni claims his classificatory criteria relate to many key aspects of organizations.

f However, Etzioni argues that the mechanism by which congruent compliance structures develop is efficiency. It might be asked: efficient for whom?

g It has also been argued that Etzioni defines the two variables in his scheme in terms of each other and that it is therefore tautologous.

h The empirical utility of the classification has been questioned.

Answer SAQ 3

a Woodward argues that organizations display different structural 'shapes' or configurations.

b These, she claims, are related to the technology of the companies.

c Three types of technological process are isolated: small batch and unit production, large batch and mass production, and process.

d A number of structural characteristics are claimed to be related to these types of technology.

e Woodward considers that the goals of the organization are important – through technology – determinants of organizational structure.

f Hickson *et al.* found that Woodward's suggested relationship between technology and organizational structure was only relevant to features of organizational structure that are most directly concerned with technology.

g Perrow also stresses the importance of technology as a determinant of organizational structure, but lays particular emphasis on the routineness of the work and the nature of reactions to exceptional cases. He therefore stresses the nature of the organization's raw material.

h Perrow thus refines and modifies Woodward's conceptualization of technology.

Answer SAQ 4

a It is difficult to know what the goals of an organization are, despite the public relations, or 'front' activities of organizational personnel.

b Groups within organizations seek different, conflicting goals.

c Organizational goals may vary over time.

d Who is it that 'knows' the goals of an organization?

e Organizational structure is not simply designed and sustained to attain organizational goals.

f Organizational goals are important for their legitimating functions.

g Organizational structure is an ever changing emergent product of intra-organizational bargaining and compromise.

Answer SAQ 5

The answers to this will depend upon your particular circumstances. Simply try to apply the main points in Section 7 to your own experience.

Answer SAQ 6

a From Max Weber on, sociologists interested in studying organizations have suggested that organizations display more than one control/authority system.

b The two types have been, as Hickson (1973) points out in his article, variously named. But they have been described with remarkable agreement as rule-bound and centralized and relatively rule-less and decentralized.

c The two types are often seen as employing different sorts of personnel.

d Some evidence for an apparent difference in organizational control structures is available.

e However, it is also argued that the amount of discretionary freedom in so-called decentralized organizations may be more apparent than real.

f Members of decentralized organizations are controlled in such ways as to ensure that they do not abuse their freedom from formal control mechanisms. Such insidious control can be of various sorts and would include the sort of training and socialization experienced by professionals.

References

AIKEN, M. and HAGE, J. (1970) 'Organizational Alienation: A Comparative Analysis' in GRUSKY and MILLER (eds) pp. 517–26.

ALBROW, M. (1973) 'The Study of Organizations – Objectivity or Bias?' in SALAMAN and THOMPSON (eds) pp. 396–413.

ARGYRIS, C. (1973) 'Peter Blau' in SALAMAN and THOMPSON (eds) pp. 76–90.

BENSMAN, J. and ROSENBERG, B. (1960) 'The Meaning of Work in Bureaucratic Society' in STEIN, M., VIDICH, A. and MANNING-WHITE, D. (eds) *Identity and Anxiety*, New York, The Free Press, pp. 181–97.

BITTNER, E. (1973) 'The Concepts of Organization' in SALAMAN and THOMPSON (eds) pp. 264–76.

BLAU, P. M. (1963) *The Dynamics of Bureaucracy*, Chicago, University of Chicago Press, second edition (set book).

BLAU, P. M. (1970a) 'The Comparative Study of Organizations' in GRUSKY and MILLER (eds) pp. 175–86.

BLAU, P. M. (1970b) 'Decentralization in Bureaucracies' in ZALD, MAYER (ed) *Power in Organizations*, Nashville, Tennessee, Vanderbilt University Press, pp. 150–74.

BLAU, P. M. and SCHOENHERR, R. A. (1971) *The Structure of Organizations*, New York, Basic Books.

BLAU, P. M. and SCHOENHERR, R. A. (1973) 'New Forms of Power' in SALAMAN and THOMPSON (eds) pp. 13–24.

BLAU, P. M. and SCOTT, R. W. (1963) *Formal Organizations: A Comparative Approach*, London, Routledge and Kegan Paul.

BURNS, T. (1967) 'The Comparative Study of Organizations' in VROOM, V. (ed) *Methods of Organizational Research*, Pittsburgh, University of Pittsburgh Press, pp. 113–70.

BURNS, T. and STALKER, G. M. (1961) *The Management of Innovation*, London, Tavistock.

BORGES, J. L. (1972) *A Personal Anthology*, London, Pan Books.

CHILD, J. (1972) 'Organizational Structure, Environment and Performance: The Role of Strategic Choice' in *Sociology*, Vol. 6, pp. 1–22.

CHILD, J. (1973) 'Organizational Structure, Environment and Performance: The Role of Strategic Choice' in SALAMAN and THOMPSON (eds) pp. 91–107.

CHOMSKY, N. (1971) *At War With Asia*, London, Fontana.

CICOUREL, A. V. (1958) 'The Front and Back of Organizational Leadership' in *Pacific Sociological Review*, Vol. 1, pp. 54–8.

COTGROVE, S. and BOX, S. (1970) *Science, Industry and Society*, London, Allen and Unwin.

CROZIER, M. (1964) *The Bureaucratic Phenomenon*, London, Tavistock.

DOSTOYEVSKY, F. M. (1972) *Notes from Underground*, translated by COULSON, J., Harmondsworth, Penguin.

DURKHEIM, E. (1938) *The Rules of Sociological Method*, New York, The Free Press.

EHRENREICH, B. and EHRENREICH, J. (1971) *The American Health Empire: Power, Profits and Politics*, New York, Vintage Books.

ETZIONI, A. (1961) *The Comparative Analysis of Complex Organizations*, Glencoe, New York, The Free Press.

ETZIONI, A. (1970) 'Compliance Theory' in GRUSKY and MILLER (eds) pp. 103–26.

ETZIONI, A. (1970) 'Two Approaches to Organizational Analysis: A Critique and a Suggestion' in GRUSKY and MILLER (eds) pp. 215–25.

FOX, A. (1973) 'The Social Organization of Industrial Work' in SALAMAN and THOMPSON (eds) pp. 321–30.

GOULDNER, A. W. (1954) *Patterns of Industrial Bureaucracy*, Kent, Ohio, Antioch Press.

GOULDNER, A. W. (1959) 'Organizational Analysis' in MERTON, R. K., BROOM, L. and COTTRELL, L. S. (eds) *Sociology Today: Problems and Prospects*, New York, Harper, pp. 400–28.

GROSS, E. (1969) 'The Definition of Organizational Goals' in *British Journal of Sociology*, Vol. XX, No. 3, pp. 277–94.

GRUSKY, O. and MILLER, G. A. (eds) (1970) *The Sociology of Organizations: Basic Studies*, New York, The Free Press (set book).

HAGE, J. and AIKEN, M. (1967) 'Relationship of Centralization to Other Structural Properties' in *Administrative Science Quarterly*, Vol. 12, pp. 72–92.

HAGE, J. and AIKEN, M. (1972) 'Routine Technology, Social Structure and Organizational Goals' in HALL, R. (ed) *The Formal Organization*, New York, Basic Books, pp. 55–72.

HALL, R. H. (1963) 'The Concept of Bureaucracy' in *American Journal of Sociology*, Vol. 69, pp. 32–40.

HALL, R. H. (ed) (1972a) *The Formal Organization*, New York, Basic Books.

HALL, R. H. (1972b) *Organizations: Structure and Process*, Englewood Cliffs, Prentice-Hall.

HALL, R. H. (1973) 'Professionalization and Bureaucratization' in SALAMAN and THOMPSON (eds) pp. 120–33.

HALL, R. H., HAAS, E. and JOHNSON, N. (1967) 'An Examination of the Blau-Scott and Etzioni Typologies' in *Administrative Science Quarterly*, Vol. 12, pp. 118–39.

HEILBRONER, R. (1970) 'How the Pentagon Rules Us' in *New York Review of Books*, July 23, pp. 5–8. This article is a review of MELMAN, S. (1970) *Pentagon Capitalism: The Political Economy of War*, New York, McGraw-Hill.

HICKSON, D. J. (1973) 'A Convergence in Organization Theory' in SALAMAN and THOMPSON (eds) pp. 108–19.

HICKSON, D. J., PUGH, D. S. and PHEYSEY, D. C. (1972) 'Operations Technology and Organizations Structure: An Empirical Reappraisal' in AZUMI, K. and HAGE, J. (eds) *Organizational Systems*, Lexington, Mass., Heath, pp. 137–50.

LENIN, V. I. (1970) *The State and Revolution*, Peking, Foreign Languages Press.

MICHELS, R. (1970) 'Oligarchy' in GRUSKY and MILLER (eds) pp. 25–43.

MILLER, G. A. (1970) 'Professionals in Bureaucracy: Alienation Among Industrial Scientists and Engineers' in GRUSKY and MILLER (eds) pp. 503–15.

MILLS, C. W. (1940) 'Situated Actions and Vocabularies of Motive' in *American Sociological Review*, Vol. 5, pp. 904–13.

MOUZELIS, N. P. (1967) *Organizations and Bureaucracy*, London, Routledge and Kegan Paul.

PARSONS, T. (1970) 'Social Systems' in GRUSKY and MILLER (eds) pp. 75–82.

PERROW, C. (1961) 'The Analysis of Goals in Complex Organizations' in *American Sociological Review*, Vol. 26, pp. 854–66.

PERROW, C. (1972a) 'A Framework for the Comparative Analysis of Complex Organizations' in BRINERHOFF, M. B. and KUNZ, P. R. (eds) *Complex Organizations and Their Environments*, Dubuque, Iowa, William C. Brown, pp. 48–67.

PERROW, C. (1972b) *Complex Organizations: A Critical Essay*, Illinois, Scott, Foresman.

PERROW, C. (1973) 'The Neo-Weberian Model: Decision Making, Conflict and Technology' in SALAMAN and THOMPSON (eds) pp. 281–92.

PUGH, D. S. and HICKSON, D. J. (1973) 'The Comparative Study of Organizations' in SALAMAN and THOMPSON (eds) pp. 50–66.

PUGH, D. S., HICKSON, D. J. and HININGS, C. R. (1971) *Writers on Organizations*, Harmondsworth, Penguin.

SALAMAN, G. and THOMPSON, K. (eds) (1973) *People and Organizations*, London, Longmans (the Reader).

SELZNICK, P. (1966) *TVA and the Grass Roots: A Study in the Sociology of Formal Organization*, New York, Harper.

SILLS, D. L. (1970) 'Preserving Organizational Goals' in GRUSKY and MILLER (eds) pp. 227–36.

SILVERMAN, D. (1970) *The Theory of Organizations*, London, Heinemann (set book).

STINCHCOMBE, A. L. (1970) 'Bureaucratic and Craft Administration of Production' in GRUSKY and MILLER (eds) pp. 261–71.

STRAUSS, A. *et al.* (1973) 'The Hospital and Its Negotiated Order' in SALAMAN and THOMPSON (eds) pp. 303–20.

STUDENTS FOR A DEMOCRATIC SOCIETY (1972) 'The Military-Industrial Complex' from the Port Huron Statement in PERROW, C. (ed) *The Radical Attack on Business*, New York, Harcourt Brace Jovanovich, pp. 15–16.

THOMPSON, J. and MCEWEN, W. (1973) 'Organizational Goals and Environment: Goal-Setting as an Interaction Process' in SALAMAN and THOMPSON (eds) pp. 155–67.

UDY, S. (1959) 'Bureaucracy and Rationality in Weber's Organizational Theory: An Empirical Study' in *American Sociological Review*, Vol. 24, pp. 791–5.

WOODWARD, J. (1969) 'Management and Technology' in BURNS, T. (ed) *Industrial Man*, Harmondsworth, Penguin, pp. 196–231.

WOODWARD, J. (1970) 'Technology and Organization' in GRUSKY and MILLER (eds) pp. 273–90.

Acknowledgements

Grateful acknowledgement is made to the following sources for material used in these units:

Text

Tavistock Publications Ltd for T. Burns and G. M. Stalker, *The Management of Innovation*.

Figures

Figure 1: The American Sociological Association and Professor Charles Perrow for C. Perrow, 'A framework for the comparative analysis of organizations' in *American Sociological Review*, 32, April 1967, pp. 194–208.

Notes

Notes

M. C. Escher, *Ascending and Descending*, Escher Foundation
Haags Gemeentemuseum – The Hague

Section cover: *Ascending and Descending,* lithograph, 1960, 38 x 28.5 cm
The endless stairs which are the main motif of this picture were taken from an article
by L. S. and R. Penrose in the February, 1958 issue of the British Journal of Psychology.
A rectangular inner courtyard is bounded by a building that is roofed in by a never-
ending stairway. The inhabitants of these living-quarters would appear to be monks,
adherents of some unknown sect. Perhaps it is their ritual duty to climb those stairs
for a few hours each day. It would seem that when they get tired they are allowed
to turn about and go downstairs instead of up. Yet both directions, though not without
meaning, are equally useless. Two recalcitrant individuals refuse, for the time being,
to take any part in this exercise. They have no use for it at all, but no doubt sooner
or later they will be brought to see the error of their nonconformity. From
The Graphic Work of M. C. Escher, written by the artist.

Contents Unit 6

Reading for this unit

You should try to read the following in parallel with this unit. You will also find references to them in the text of the unit. (For full references see References at the end of the unit.)

1 David Silverman, *The Theory of Organizations,* chapters 1–5 (set book).

2 Amitai Etzioni, 'Two Approaches to Organizational Analysis: A Critique and a Suggestion' in Oscar Grusky and George A. Miller (eds) *The Sociology of Organizations* (set book) pp. 215–25.

3 Talcott Parsons, 'Social Systems' in Grusky and Miller (eds) pp. 75–82. You should have already looked at this as part of the background reading to Units 4 and 5.

4 Daniel Katz and Robert L. Kahn, 'Open-Systems Theory' in Grusky and Miller (eds) pp. 149–58.

5 Fritz J. Roethlisberger and William J. Dickson, 'Human Relations' in Grusky and Miller (eds) pp. 53–63.

6 Walter Buckley, 'Society as a Complex Adaptive System' in Graeme Salaman and Kenneth Thompson (eds) *People and Organizations* (the Reader) pp. 134–54.

7 J. Eldridge, 'Systems Analysis and Industrial Behaviour' (offprint in the Supplementary Material accompanying this unit, see Section 4 for a discussion of this).

8 F. E. Emery and E. L. Trist, 'Socio-Technical Systems' (offprint in the Supplementary Material accompanying this unit, see Section 4 for a discussion of this).

The organization as a system

> . . . from the commencement of my managements, I have viewed the population with a mechanism and every part of the establishment as a system composed of many parts, and which it was my duty and interest to combine, so that every hand as well as every spring, lever, and wheel should effectively co-operate to produce the greatest pecuniary gain to the proprietors. (Robert Owen 1813, quoted in Cleland and King 1972 p. 80.)

Objectives

To introduce the student to the various types of systems approach and identify their relation to the theory of organizations.

Summary

General systems theory purports to cover all types of system and leans heavily on cybernetic, biological or organic analogies. We look first at the concept of goals, since this is central to systems and cybernetic concepts, and show that in the case of social systems, the goals are more complex and fragmented than in physical systems. The student is shown that a simple equilibrium model does not suffice and that organizations display a *managed* equilibrium rather than an automatic stability.

Systems analysis using the concepts of inputs and outputs provides an introduction to methods for identifying the factors that must be managed in order for the system to be controlled.

Two systems models, which help to identify important interactions and interfaces, are introduced, leading to the construction of a general systems model.

Finally, the cybernetic approach is reviewed, concentrating first on its organic origins. We then introduce the modern cybernetic approach which attempts to accommodate the non-deterministic action approach, by emphasis on the generation of interpretations and meaning structures.

The main object of this unit is to raise the question – can we study organizations as systems? What are the limitations of this approach? What assumption does the systems perspective make about the nature of organizations?

For example, it is possible to consider organizations as in some way similar to biological organisms: this approach can be criticized for stressing the equilibrium aspect, which is not necessarily strong in organizations, and ignoring conflict. We can also view organizations as simply complex arrangements of interacting entities which have fixed operational responses, with behaviour determined by the inputs to the network. This can be criticized as too mechanistic or as being dangerously close to reductionism. Similarly, the concept of an organization as a sentient being with a simple goal of its own, can be criticized as ignoring the variety of its human components – and as being dangerously similar to reification. The abstract entity, the system, has no goals – but the individual actors, whose relationships in the system make up the system, have goals, and maybe these unite into a single consensually held goal. Or maybe the sub-systems have a multitude of goals, the net outcome of interactions and conflicts resulting in the final direction or behaviour of the overall system or organization.

This more complex picture is perhaps more realistic: it depends on interaction, communication and perception, as well as the idea that behaviour is a direct response to inputs or stimuli.

Discussion of these various criticisms will help clarify our understanding of organizations and raise a number of questions. Can we expect organizations constantly to maintain equilibrium or will they naturally tend towards chaos, unless controlled? Is conflict endemic, healthy or deviant? How strong are the effects of various factors both internal and external impinging on sub-systems in the organization? Can we understand the problem of *control* by studying the effects of these various factors? Can we use the idea of information flow and perception as a help in explaining the individual's and groups' formation of attitudes and expectations and interpretation of reality in organization?

Introduction to systems theory
General systems theory

Systems theory has become a popular unifying approach in many different disciplines. In the biological sciences it has been used to describe the functioning at cellular level of organic material; in the physical sciences, under the name 'systems engineering' or 'control engineering' or 'cybernetics', it has been used to describe the flow of information in complex electronic/mechanical systems. In thermo-dynamics we talk of open and closed systems and entropy.

A general systems theory has been advanced which purports to explain the behaviour of any system.

Does this include social systems, and in particular, organizations? Can the sociologist use any of these ideas?

To answer these questions we need to know a little more about systems analysis, and the systems approach. Then we can see how (or if) the general theory applies to the study of organizations.

Systems theory

What do we mean by a system?

There are many definitions of what constitutes a system. Basically any group of entities which are functionally interdependent can be called a system. Any group of entities which are interrelated so as to perform some function, or reach some goal, can be seen to be acting as a system.

Let us briefly examine some simple systems concepts, which will be of use in our discussion.

Large systems usually contain sub-systems, which ideally work independently towards the final goal of the major system. This picture of a hierarchy of systems and sub-systems represents a systems model. By studying the interrelations between sub-systems we can learn something of the nature of the system. Similarly we can identify components of the system or sub-system – the next level down in the hierarchy, and we can study the interaction between these. No system is entirely closed or self-contained. It must exist in an environment and must interact with that environment to some extent. We say that such a system is *open*. We can talk about inputs and outputs to the system from and to the environment: and we may be able to define the system's boundary across which these inputs and outputs pass – that is the boundary between the system and its environment. We can try to define the system's environment by suggesting that it affects the functioning of the system (by constraints or imperatives) but is not *part* of the system – it does not share the system's *goals*. Probably the most popular systems concept is, of course, feedback. Many systems are structured so that some part of their output response is fed back to become an input. The system monitors its own behaviour through this feedback loop. The feedback concept derives from electrical control systems and has proved an invaluable tool in general systems analysis. These concepts – systems, sub-systems, goal, systems model, input, output, feedback, system boundary and environment, will be followed up in more detail in a later section, dealing with a number of systems models.

Definitions of system

Sub-systems

Systems model

System components

Environment
Inputs and outputs

Boundary

Feedback

The systems approach

Is the systems approach a particular theory or simply a methodology which has much in common with sociological analysis?

I would suggest that the systems approach is a way of thinking which enables us to cope with complex phenomena by identifying their systemic relations. Once we realize that the structure we are studying displays the properties of a system we may be in a position to identify crucial goals, linkages or controlling factors in its structure and functioning. The analytical process typical of systems analysis can lay bare the interrelationships between sub-systems and their inputs and outputs, and may focus our attention on unexpected feedback loops, behavioural lags, delays in response to particular inputs, or crucial interactions between inputs or sub-systems. The systems concept ensures that we look for these linkages since we are aware that the structure we are studying is an interdependent arrangement of sub-systems.

Helps identify key factors

In the next section we will ask specifically what these generalizations about systems structure have to offer us in the study of organizations, and in particular concentrate on two systems' concepts – goals and equilibrium.

1 Organization models

1.1 Organizations as systems

How can organizations be analysed as systems?

Certainly an organization can be thought of as having identifiable goals, with its sub-parts acting in concert to reach these objectives. Parsons defined an organization as a 'special type of social system organized about the primacy of interest in the attainment of a particular type of system goal'. (1970 p. 76.)

System goal

SAQ 1 What do we 'miss out' when we view organizations as having one united goal?

The fact that organizations have human components introduces a degree of variety and internal inconsistency to the mechanical model of a functioning system. But the systems approach is, to some extent, capable of coping with this individual variety in organizations, by focusing not on individuals, but on their arrangement in the system. In the strict sense of the word, organizations are arrangements of people or roles. We can study how this system behaves, changes, handles events and processes information. Now such a system can be seen to be arranged for some purpose – it has a goal. Systems analysis however should reveal that there are, in the systems arrangement, sub-systems which may be formally ascribed a different role or may develop, autonomously, different roles – and goals. Sociologists usually label these autonomous developments informal as opposed to formal, organization.

So human sub-systems, sub-groups of people, may have goals which differ from or are even contradictory to the stated goal of the major system. And of course the overall system's goals may be complex. The stated goals of the organization may differ from the real operating goals or they may not be consistent in functional terms. It is often suggested that competitive organizations have profit or growth as their major goal, but this is often qualified by the secondary goal of 'benefiting the people who work in the organization and the society which the organization serves'. These two goals are not necessarily adhered to simultaneously – they represent different views of the systems.

Multiple goals model

Social sub-systems, such as work-groups, office groups, etc., internalize goals in terms of norms which again may or may not be in the interests of the overall system. Industrial sociology provides many examples of restrictive work group norms, developed by the group to defend and advance the group as opposed to the organization.

Albrow identifies some of these latent sub-systems goals:

> It is a characteristic of social action that no objective is 'given' in isolation from other objectives. The limits on the attainment of an objective are set not only by the availability of means but also by criteria which determine what means are acceptable. These criteria frequently stem from goals which are independent of the objective from which the analysis

began. Thus managers may well have goals other than high production e.g. profit, industrial peace, the preservation of power and privilege . . . (p. 398.)

... Members of the organization may put job-security at the very centre of the organizational goal structure, and commitment to any other goal may be regarded as a price to be paid. Alternatively, it may be the case that an organizational goal is treated by the various social groupings in the organization as purely instrumental in obtaining their own purposes. (Albrow 1973 p. 406.)

Simon (1945) points out that decisions and goals are generated according to the individuals' limited perception of reality – rather than in a full, objective knowledge of the situation. Inevitably, the individual can only perceive some part of the system that surrounds him. He must operate within what Simon calls a 'bounded rationality' based on a simplified mental model of the system.[1] It is in terms of this model that the individual makes decisions. One of the objects of the systems approach is to expand this mental model.

1.2 Organization goals

System analysis, as applied to mechanical and cybernetic systems, lays strong emphasis on the definition, and preferably quantification, of a precise goal, as an essential first step in any analysis of a system. As we have seen, however, when we try to analyse the more complex *social* systems, such as organizations, this process is not so straightforward, and we may have to adopt 'multiple goal' models, with different goals operating at different levels. (Mesarovic *et al.* 1973.) It is useful, generally, to look at the interaction between the goals at different levels, for example, between the goals of sub-systems and the goals of the system as a whole.

In the case of organizations, goal analysis is well established. Indeed we often define organizations by their goals (as in the quote at the beginning of Section 1.1). An organization is seen as a co-ordinated body (or system) of individuals (and perhaps machines) arranged to reach some goal or perform some function or service. Etzioni provides a useful summary of this type of systems argument (1970). In this section we will spend some time reviewing the various propositions concerning the goals of organizations and of the individuals in them. We hope to illustrate the diversity of goals that exist in organizations. Of course we must be careful about what type of organization we are considering. Commercial and industrial organizations are obviously economic organizations and one would expect economic goals to be important for them. However, since all organizations exist in a competitive environment the economic constraints may often be important even though the organization's stated objective is something else.

The traditional economic model of organizations stresses the goal of profit maximization. All other goals are viewed as secondary. Since profit maximization is apparently central, it is worth studying this goal further.

The general economic theory of the market economy suggests that the economic organization (or firm) strives to maximize its profits. In the (ideal) case of perfect and free competition this means that the consumer has control, since he can choose amongst rival brands and thus direct the production in his interests. Theoretically, consumer sovereignty would mean instant feedback to the producing firm. In reality however, there are severe lags in this feedback, and modern production techniques require substantial lead times before they can switch production in response to consumer choice. Similarly there is an inertia in the labour market. And there is, in fact, imperfect competition, monopoly and oligopoly, as well as some degree of control by the organization over the market environment.

Economic goals

SAQ 2 Do you think 'profit maximization' is the major goal of economic organizations?

1 Cyert and March (1963) call this a 'local rationality' and suggest that the decision making is carried out in terms of 'satisfactory' solutions, rather than 'optimum' ones.

Modern economic organizations plan their production and attempt to control the market through advertizing. We therefore have a partially planned market society. The degree to which the economic organization *can* direct the market of course varies: in totally planned societies (e.g. USSR) the steering is (theoretically, at least) absolute: demand is totally managed by the economic organization (in this case, the state). According to Galbraith (1967), the type of 'planning' (the 'guided market economy') we have in the West, means that 'profit maximization' is not necessarily the only important goal. It might prove expedient, rather, to secure control over demand, to stabilize the market or defend territory. Growth of production and expansion of markets may be important goals – but the simple optimization of profit is not significant in a planned market economy as in a perfectly competitive market economy. Also, as Child (1973) points out, the controllers of modern economic organizations have some freedom to choose policies and goals other than those determined by the nature of the market or the technology. Thus, according to Galbraith, the company finds that if it can establish a certain adequate level of profit and if this can be stabilized, then other goals become more significant. A similar denial of 'profit maximization' as the major goal comes from H. Simon, who records the common management view that 'the goal of business is not profit but efficient production of goods and services'. (1969 p. 162.) He suggests that profit maximization is only really possible if one subscribes to the 'economic' model of the omniscient super-rational entrepreneur. (Simon 1945.) The manager in practice cannot possibly review all possible behaviour alternatives before making a decision. Therefore he must be content with 'satisficing' rather than 'maximizing' and he looks for a course of action that is satisfactory or 'good enough'!

The changing nature of management, as ownership and control are increasingly separated and professional specialization increases, has also been seen as likely to contribute to a lessening in importance of the profit motive. Galbraith suggests that modern corporations are increasingly governed by professional 'technicians' – economists, financiers, systems analysts, technologists, market researchers, who comprise a 'technostructure'. He suggests this new 'class' has the goal of survival, efficiency and control rather than of 'profit maximization'.

In making this type of assertion, we move from the level of the organization to that of the individual. There are both personal goals, dependent on the motivations of the individual, and professional goals, which depend on the organizational roles of the individual. In the vast modern organizations, it is unlikely that the individual will see the company's profit maximization as directly relating to his own welfare – it is a distant goal. Nor is his professional role and decision making activity directly linked to profit. His personal objectives may be to maximize his own salary, secure his own position and expand his influence. His desire for job security is often a crucial influence on his decision making. As Burns and Stalker (1961) have mentioned, the efforts expended by executives in business organizations in defence of and advancement of their career prospects, are considerable. We might even suggest that successful careerism becomes a goal in itself. Burns and Stalker point out that 'the hierarchical order of rank and power realized in the organization chart, that prevails in all organizations, is both a control system and a career ladder'. (1961 p. xii.) The internal struggles and political intrigue that these career goals involve may of course absorb so much effort, as to be dysfunctional (i.e. not in the best interests of the organization).

Summarizing, we have reviewed the wide range and multiplicity of goals that can be attributed to organizations and have attempted to illustrate the argument that profit maximization in commercial enterprises is perhaps no longer the central goal. What we are faced with is a *system* which operates according to complex interrelated sub-goals, as is discussed by Etzioni (1970). This multiple-goal model does not however necessarily deny the significance of profit as a goal: it simply suggests that there are a number of functional requirements which a system must meet, if it is to

Security and equilibrium goals

Individual goals

Summary

maintain some kind of stability and equilibrium.

> . . . the decision-making mechanism is a loosely coupled system in which the profit constraint is only one among a number of constraints and enters into most sub-systems only in indirect ways. It would be both legitimate and realistic to describe most business firms as directed towards profit making – subject to a number of side constraints – operating through a network of decision-making processes that introduces many gross approximations into the search for profitable courses of action. Further, the goal ascription does not imply that any employee is motivated by the firm's profit goal, although some may be. (Simon 1969 p. 174.)

It is unlikely however that those not ascribing to the profit goal would be given access to power and influence in an organization. As a manager of General Motors has said:

> The management, in its delegation of authority, is bound to make certain to the best of its ability that authority will be used in accordance with the interests of the business. This precludes it from delegating authority to anyone whose interests may be in conflict with those of the owners of the business. (Chamberlain 1948 p. 17.)

This serves as a reminder that economic organizations have a power structure that affects the weight given to various goals.

SAQ 3 How can the system approach help us to take sub-goals into account?

Thus an organization cannot be viewed on a simple organic or cybernetic model as a unified structure maintaining equilibrium through goal-directed behaviour. The equilibrium of an organization is a result of the balancing and managing of complex internal tensions and conflicts, and its goal is not a unified shared one, but emerges generally as a compromise from the interaction of multiple constraints.[1]

1.3 Equilibrium models

The concept of equilibrium is important to systems thinking. Concepts of equilibrium, however, that draw too heavily on an organic model of a self-adapting, self-equilibrating system can be criticized, for reasons suggested in the previous section, as being inadequate for the purposes of organizational analysis. We will look briefly first at a systems theory drawing heavily on an organic-equilibrium model, before considering some systems concepts and models that revolve more round notions of *managed* rather than natural equilibrium, and that seem more appropriate to organizational analysis.

Parsons' theory of social systems

Parsons has developed a systems theory which has been widely accepted and used in the study both of society in general and of organizations. Parsons' idea of a social system is that it functions so as to constantly adjust itself internally to a state of equilibrium. Any particular input – be it personnel or structural change – is coped with by the sub-systems, and a new equilibrated system evolved.

Parsons talks in terms of behaviour or 'actions' which are either *functional* or *dysfunctional* – that is actions which produce either helpful or unhelpful consequences of the goals of the system. He suggests however that dysfunctional behaviour will inevitably be modified so as not to disrupt the self-equilibrating tendencies of the system. If this does not occur the system will lose all equilibrium and degenerate: 'while parts of the system may not serve the goal (i.e. may be dysfunctional) these will in the long run become modified so as to serve the system or will "disengage" themselves from it. If neither event occurs the system will "degenerate".' (Silverman 1970 p. 31.)

---

1 Cyert and March (1963) have produced a 'behavioural theory of the firm' which describes this process of resolving conflicts and reaching a temporary 'coalition of interests'.

Parsons tackles the problem of why organized activities in society are stable and continue, despite changes in personnel. His approach leads to a, perhaps, one-sided view that what is central to the 'social system' is its stability – its constant striving towards equilibrium. Hence conflict in society and in organizations is relegated to secondary importance, as is also the phenomenon of change, that so often accompanies conflict.

What Parsons is attempting is a *general* 'theory of society', illustrating how the various parts of the social system function in order to maintain equilibrium. He is attempting to link the ideas of 'normative control', 'shared cultural conditioning', private and public interests, etc., into a 'grand theory'. (See Parsons 1970.)

Conflict, change and deviance

As we have noted, Parsons' insistence on 'consensus' and 'equilibrium' has been widely criticized for failing to deal with 'change', 'deviance' and 'conflict'.

But we cannot afford to ignore deviant behaviour in our analysis. Thus deviant activities must be included as part of the system and not as residual and dysfunctional. Deviance, and conflict produced by deviance may be important *functional* components of the systems of organizations: 'Conflict, rather than being disruptive and dissociating may indeed be a means of balancing and hence maintaining a society as a going concern . . .' (p. 137.) 'A flexible society benefits from conflict because such behaviour, by helping to create and modify norms, assures its continuance under changed conditions.' (Coser 1956 p. 154.)

The idea of equilibrium is still of course retained in this formulation. More radical conflict theorists would suggest that the changes that ensue might totally restructure the organization so that the concept of equilibrium or even of dynamic equilibrium would be inappropriate. We will see in later sections that open systems are characterized by the capability to restructure and adapt themselves in this way continuously in response to changes in their environment. These changes relate not only to straightforward changes in (for example) market conditions or technological innovations, but also changes in social and cultural values. Open systems theorists, in contrast to Parsonian system theorists, do not see organizational adaptation as being necessarily of a self-equilibrating nature. The way in which an organization adapts to its environment is quite frequently *planned* or *managed* – although of course, unconscious adaptations do also occur, particularly in the sphere of social and cultural values.

Organizational change

1.4 Inputs and outputs

One of the most useful systems' methodologies is to study the inputs and outputs of a system. What are the possible inputs and outputs to and from an organization?

Taking the case of an industrial organization, in summary, the inputs might be:

1 personnel
2 their attitudes and expectations
3 targets, constraints and imperatives from the environment (e.g. the market)
4 raw materials, equipment, techniques.

The obvious output is the product of the organization – be it physical or abstract, i.e. what it does – its function.

But there are other outputs – which feed back to affect the functioning of the system. The *behavioural response* of the people in the organization can be seen as an output. It may be in the form of actual action or it may be simply attitudinal. Adverse attitudes (boredom, dissatisfaction, etc.) may lead to action (strikes, absenteeism, labour turnover, etc.).

Behaviour *in* the system may be determined by both the inputs from the environment and the conditions inside the system. Industrial sociologists talk of technology and job design affecting the behaviour of workers: external market pressures also may affect them. There are many other factors such as the payment system, the strength of the union, etc., that may affect behaviour in the organization.

These input and output factors are summarized on the 'Systems Diagram' (Figure 1), which we will introduce after we have described two systems models which separate some of these factors – the socio-technical system model and the open system model.

1.5 Emergence of the socio-technical model

The work of Elton Mayo at the Hawthorne plant of the Western Electric Company represents an early example of a systems approach to organizations. Like most early systems work, it tended to view systems as closed or isolated groups of interacting sub-units, ignoring any inputs that might come in from outside the systems boundary. The article by Mayo's associates, Roethlisberger and Dickson (1970), will give you an idea of the approach: note in particular their reliance on the concept of equilibrium.

The work group was seen as a stable sub-system which had both formal and informal interactions. The formal structure depends on the actual task in hand and on the supervisory system. The informal system – which Mayo concentrated on – depends on interpersonal relationships, friendship, group loyalties and group defence. This accent on 'human relations' can be compared with the bias towards task-related interactions typical of the more sophisticated *socio-technical* systems, which incorporated the technological environment of the work group into the model. The prescriptions made by the human relations theorists involved improving communications and consideration of informal group norms and loyalties. The socio-technical school (Emery, Trist *et al.*), while not denying the importance of informal group interactions, concentrate on the aspects of these interactions that are in some way determined by and interrelated with the task in hand.

Thus Emery and Trist (1969) see the shop-floor sub-system as being neither a purely technical system nor a purely social system, but as an interdependent socio-technical system. They developed this concept as a result of research into the effects of technological change in coal mines and elsewhere. (This work is described in the offprint in the Supplementary Material accompanying this unit.) The essence of the socio-technical approach has been aptly summarized as follows:

> The technological demands place limits on the type of work organization possible, but the work organization has social, psychological properties of its own that are independent of the technology. From this point of view, it makes as little sense to regard social relationships as being determined by the technology as it does to regard the manner in which a job is performed as being determined by the socio-psychological characteristics of the workers. The crucial implication of this theory was that the attainment of optimum conditions for either aspect does not necessarily result in optimum conditions for the system as a whole. Indeed the optimization of the whole may well require a less than optimum state for each separate aspect. (Pugh *et al.* 1971 pp. 50-1.)

Emery and Trist thus denied that socio-technical systems had self-adapting equilibrating tendencies; these systems must be consciously planned and matched if optimization of performance is to be attained. Given a suitable design of socio-technical system, then of course interdependent self-regulation *may* be possible: the system may be self-managing.

SAQ 4 What role does informal interpersonal 'friendship' have in shop floor work groups, if we accept the 'socio-technical' model?

1.6 Open systems

The open systems approach attempts to include influences from outside the immediate work-group environment, which the socio-technical approach tends to ignore. It is also used to refer to the effects of inputs, derived from the organization's environment, on the organization as a whole (e.g. a firm).

Includes outside influences

On this type of model, the system is seen as open – that is sensitive to its environment. This environment also includes other systems which may interact: 'The organization, i.e. the whole complex of interrelated and encapsulated sub-units, groups and individuals, has to adapt to a changing world which includes other groups and organizations such as shareholders, customers, trade unions and governments.' (Lupton 1971 p. 122.)

Fundamentally, the open system is one in which materials, information, attitudes, etc., are imported and exported across the system's boundary. This boundary can be drawn anywhere for the purpose of analysis. If the system one is studying is the whole organization then the boundary is between the organization and its external environment; if the system being studied is the work-group, then the boundary is between this group and the rest of the organization, which in this case is its environment.

Boundaries

According to the concept of entropy, it is, in fact, impossible for any system to remain *closed*, if it is to survive. Although we can treat some systems as 'closed' for the purpose of analysis, strictly speaking all systems are open. Here we are making an analogy to certain physical systems – usually studied in thermodynamics. It is axiomatic (in physics) that to perform any work a system must import energy, or else it will run down. Similarly, for a social system – such as an organization – it must import both physical materials, human operatives and attitudes, information, expectations and social sanctions.

Entropy

The organizational system thus relies on its environment to provide its requirements.

This is obvious in mechanical-material terms. It is also true in terms of the need for an enterprise to have its activities accepted (sanctioned) by the community it serves. And again we can see that the motivations and expectations of the work force (the human component of the system) are also generated in and by the 'environment', are 'brought in' to the system, and largely define the behaviour of the 'people in the organization'. (See Katz and Kahn 1970.)

Attitudes, expectations and social sanctions

As Elliott Jaques puts it:

> The factory operates within its larger society. It is successful as an industrial undertaking insofar as it succeeds in maintaining a connection between the new methods it is trying to develop and the central features and trends of the culture of this society . . . a self-sanctioning industrial organization is impossible, conformity with the larger society being enforced in innumerable ways . . . These external sanctions are to some extent carried inside the organization in each individual member of the concern . . . (Jaques 1951 p. 258.)

Bennis and Thomas argue that 'The contemporary organization must necessarily adapt to change by constantly monitoring the relevance and legitimacy of its present goals' (Bennis and Thomas 1972 p. 21) – the organization must respond to changes not only in the market but in the social and cultural environment.

This type of open systems argument should be compared with the belief, expressed by Galbraith and others, that some organizations try to control their environment and determine the 'norms' and 'values' of the society.

The modern organization is seen as necessarily open to and aware of its environment, and at the same time it is suggested that it attempts to consciously manage its environment.

Attempts to control environment

As Drucker puts it '. . . managing goes way beyond passive reaction and adaptation. It implies responsibility for attempting to shape the economic environment, for planning, initiating and carrying through changes, for constantly pushing back the limitations of economic circumstances on the enterprise's freedom of action . . .' (Drucker 1955 pp. 8–9.)

Of course we must be careful not to confuse the organization and the people inside the organization. The statements we have made so far about 'what organizations should or must do' are obviously reifications. Attitudes, expectations and imperatives impinge on individuals or groups and their response in aggregate makes up the organization's behaviour.

In particular we must try to be clear about the difference between these input effects on the controllers, or managers, and the workers. As Child has pointed out, the former group have a certain freedom to make strategic choices, and do not necessarily have to respond directly to economic or technical imperatives: they can manage or cope with the environment. (Child 1973.) Child's model thus decouples some of the behaviour of actors in the system from the input factors. Nevertheless, many of the predispositions, attitudes, and expectations of both managers and workers are generated, and perhaps determined, by these external influences. Of course, there is much debate as to whether attitudes, etc. are generated inside or outside the organization. It is nevertheless generally accepted that the attitudes and expectations generated in the wider community partially determine behaviour discernible in the organization – or at least are important factors.

Different input effects on managers and workers

Goldthorpe's study (1968) of workers in Luton car plants and their community relations, certainly indicates that the 'instrumental attitude' (emphasis on 'expected cash reward' without particular concern for conditions or friendships at work) generated *outside* the workplace dominated behaviour at work, and attitudes to work, for the particular group he studied.

Quite apart from this type of economic motivation, there are other and more complex factors which impinge on the workers in industrial organizations and which derive from the community – factors relating to the community's history, the degree of working class solidarity, the history of trade unions, the coherence of the community structure and so on. It is this type of factor that the open systems perspective asks us to consider.

1.7 Open systems and their environments

Katz and Kahn (1970) pioneered this open systems approach to organizations and their management. The modern open systems approach which they describe is currently being pursued with the aim, for example, of providing an understanding of how the managers of modern organizations can deal with and adapt to their fast changing or 'turbulent' environments. Examples of this research are Emery's (1969) work on the 'Causal Texture of Organizational Environments' and Lawrence and Lorsch's (1967) analysis. These studies represent attempts to analyse the structure of the environment in systems terms, to evolve quantitative measures of the rate of change of elements in the environment which affect the organizations. In an attempt to produce a theory of environmental and organizational change, Lawrence and Lorsch (1967) depict three analytically separate segments in the organizational environment (market, research and development, technological) which could change at different rates. This enables a more precise analysis to be made of a generally 'turbulent' environment and of the feedback relationship between this environment and intra-organizational change. For example, the rate of change of scientific developments, as explored by a Research Development department, may be very high 'while at the same time and in the same organization, the rate of change in customers' tastes or competitors' tactics might be low, and the rate of change of product or method very low.' (Lupton 1971 p. 127.) Or, to take another example, a research scientist in an organization:

Segmented environment

> . . . might not find out for years what use, if any, the organization made of his findings and whether economic benefit accrued, but the feedback of complaint or praise from customers to the marketing man may be very fast, and faster still may be the verdict on the quantity and quality of the output of a process or a production department. Plainly, the rate of change and time-spans of feedback will differ from organization to organization, as well as from segment to segment of the same organization. (Lupton 1971 p. 127.)

Earlier attempts to relate organizational structure to environment were made by Woodward (1959) and Burns and Stalker (1961). Essentially these studies highlighted the fact that certain organizational structures were suitable for different types of environment. Woodward concentrated on the technological environment, while Burns and Stalker included such features as types of product market and rates of technological changes. Neither Burns and Stalker, nor Woodward, however, conceive of the relationship between environment and organizational structures as mechanically deterministic. The perception of management, as to what seems to them to be the most suitable form of organization, is still an important mediating factor. Both research teams found organizations attempting to operate with a structure unsuitable to their environment, although they were inevitably less successful than organizations more suitably matched to their environments. The system, therefore, has to be managed – it is not self-adapting or self-equilibrating.

> The organization, with its sub-systems, groups and individuals, does not react automatically to its environment. The processes through which equilibrium is sought result from conscious decisions and activities of individuals and groups. Someone has to decide what changes have to be made in response to environmental stimuli, whether to diversify products, to purchase a new machine, to employ a personnel manager. Someone has to define new tasks and create organizational configurations.' (Lupton 1971, p. 123.)

It is precisely because the system is not self-adapting that problems of conflicting goals or strategies at different levels of the organization arise. Management strategy might run counter to the smooth adaptation of a sub-group to its environment and then there may be open conflict or resistance to change. The open system approach can be applied to this phenomenon also by drawing the system boundary round this particular sub-group and analysing this group's reaction to inputs from its surrounding environment, both inside and outside the organization. Lupton and Cunnison (1964) have made contributions in this area.

In 1.8 we attempt to draw a systems diagram illustrating these links between groups, sub-groups and their environment, in the case of an industrial organization.

1.8 Systems diagram

The analysis of systems is often assisted by the use of schematic charts. The systems diagram (Figure 1) is an attempt to illustrate the various inputs, outputs and feedback loops relating to an industrial organization and its environment – the organization being seen as an open system.

Most of the inputs and outputs have been mentioned in this unit, and you should find this diagram helpful in fitting them together into a mental picture or model.

The management sub-system co-ordinates men, machine and materials and attempts to control activities in the workshop socio-technical system. Since the system (the enterprise) is open, management is constrained by external pressures – from the shareholders and from the labour, materials and capital market. Management must also respond to pressures from the workers transmitted through the union and also as monitored directly by supervisors.

Attitudes and expectations about work, pay and conditions exist in the community and impinge on the system. Experiences gained at work also feed back to the community as does the experience of trade unionism.

Note that we have ignored the cash-flow loops (profits, wages, salaries and investment) in this diagram although we illustrate cash inputs. Obviously market pressures (from labour, resources, sales) all impinge on management and constrain their decision making as to pay scales and investment, so that market pressures affect the shop-floor system indirectly.

There are many reservations as to the viability of this type of input/output model. How can we measure inputs such as community attitudes and worker attitudes? How can we, in any particular situation, identify which input is significant? Can we

Figure 1 Systems diagram – an industrial organization as an open socio-technical system in a 'socio-economic' environment

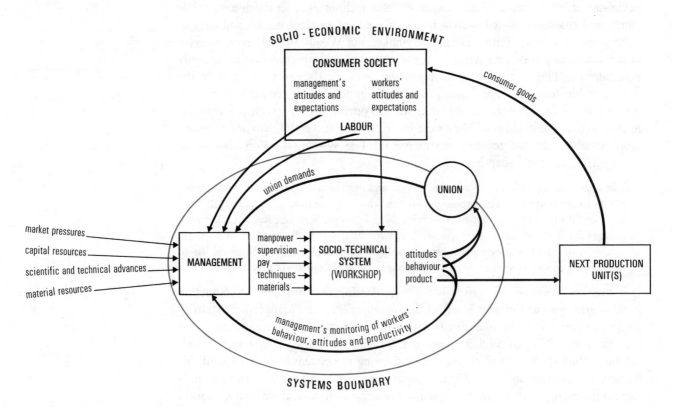

identify causal links between particular inputs, in an array of inputs, and the various outputs?

There are many techniques of statistical analysis which are of relevance to these problems. For example, if we can produce data on inputs and outputs we can attempt to test for correlations or associations between variations in these data. There are multiple regression techniques which allow us to make some kinds of statistical association between many factors, and test for causal links.

Hence it is, at least in theory, possible to identify links and relationships between the factors we have introduced on this diagram and to make a start at a formal systems analysis. Of course, such analysis is in its infancy and may well be totally unsuccessful. Industrial sociologists have explored many of these possible correlations – for example between the type of technology and worker attitude or worker behaviour. However, as we shall discuss later, more recent systems theorists suggest that it is inadequate to simply identify input factors and related output behaviour (i.e. to study the system as if it were a sealed 'black box'): what is significant is the precise mechanism through which the individual responds to inputs. They are no longer satisfied with an analysis that sees behaviour and attitudes as determined directly, in a stimulus response manner, by inputs.

1.9 Systems modelling

As we have emphasized earlier, both the open systems and the socio-technical approaches have merit. The more recent open systems perspective is an attempt to subsume the socio-technical approach, taking into account interactions with the environment of the shop-floor sub-system and with the environment of the whole organization. Thus the model, as we have seen in Figure 1, is expanded to include a multiplicity of factors which impinge on individuals in the sub-system, and does not concentrate on solely individual human factors or task-determined socio-technical factors.

You will have realized by now that there is no *one* thing called systems theory; although there may be a typical systems approach. We have outlined a number of theoretical uses of the systems concept, ranging from Parsons' equilibrium model, to the socio-technical model. Etzioni discusses some further points in his article on 'Two Approaches to Organizational Analysis' (1970). We turn now to the 'cybernetic' system approach.

As we have seen social systems can be modelled verbally, i.e. in words using logical 'argument'.

Some systems – such as mechanical, biological, electronic and operational systems – can be modelled in more formal mathematical terms. This is the basis of cybernetics: the study of systems in terms of information and control, using such physical concepts as feedback, goal-directed behaviour, automatic self-regulation, etc.

Cybernetic models

Some of these concepts can be used in the study of social systems and organizations, but there are fundamental limits to the analogy between mechanical/physical systems and social systems. Generally, this difference relates to the degree of openness of the system. For example, mechanical systems can be designed to operate relatively independently of their environments: they tend to be closed systems, and they tend to operate according to relatively well defined goals.

Thus the cybernetic approach, based on drawing analogies between biological, electronic and social systems, has fundamental limitations. These limitations also hold true for the body of thought called general systems theory which attempts to erect general models which can be used to analyse a large range of systems from social organizations to ecological systems.

1.10 Systems, organizations and organisms

The general systems approach amounts to a general taxonomy of behaviour and function across a wide range of diverse areas.

It has much in common with other generalist attempts at unifying our understanding of social, economic, and biological behaviour. So we might expect general laws, applicable for a range of different systems: 'In Cybernetics, organizational forms are studied independently of their carrier, so that, in a certain sense, cybernetic systems constitute common models of systems defined in different, frequently widely remote, scientific disciplines.' (Klir and Valach, quoted in Chadwick 1971 p. 189.)

It has been pointed out that many of these approaches rely on an analogy to natural biological organisms. The state is seen as a vast corporate body – an organism. We use the terms 'organ', 'arm' (of the law), etc., and these functionalist views derive from attempts to produce a model of society based on the analogy of the human body.

There is of course a basic philosophical point here. Why should organizations behave like individuals or organisms? Can we usefully generalize from the behaviour of one component? For example, Katz and Kahn point out that:

A caution

> . . . though various types of open system have common characteristics by virtue of being open systems, they differ in other characteristics. If this were not the case, we would be able to obtain all our basic knowledge about social organization through studying the biological organisms or even through the study of a single cell. (Katz and Kahn 1970 p. 152.)

This type of criticism is similar to that of Herbert Spencer's classic criticism of over-eager analogies between 'organisms' and 'societies': 'The social organism, discrete instead of concrete, asymmetrical instead of symmetrical, sensitive in all its units instead of having a single sensitive centre, is not comparable to any particular type of individual organism, animal or vegetable'. (Spencer 1897 p. 592.)

These critics suggest that one must be wary of reductionist attempts to disregard differences and over-reduce complexities to simple patterns and basic, generalizable, models and laws. In particular there seems to be no reason why every system should be reducible to any particular model or analogue. The defenders of the systems approach acknowledge that differences do exist and must not be glossed over, but assert that the systems approach has an important role to play in locating and analysing the precise nature of these differences. As Buckley has said: the substantive difference between systems:

> . . . lies in the way they are *organized*, in the particular mechanisms and dynamics of the interrelations among the parts and with the environment. Thus we now understand, in principle, the particular kinds of mechanisms or internal linkages of parts that must underlie any goal-seeking, or purposive behavior, whether of machine, man, or group . . . Thus, a major goal of the General Systems Research movement is to trace out just such structural similarities *and structural differences*, between 'substantively' different types of systems. (Buckley 1967 p. 3.)

While an organic model or analogy does seem to be implied by systems analysts when they use such terms as 'goal directed behaviour', 'boundary maintenance' and 'purposive behaviour', yet, as we have already indicated, few contemporary systems writers impose a totally organic self-equilibrating model on social systems. Most writers stress that social equilibrium (just as post-Keynesian economic 'equilibrium') is a managed and not a 'natural equilibrium' and that adaptive changes are usually the results of conscious decisions made by groups or individuals who happen to be in a position of power that enables them to make such decisions. Thus it is conceded that there are fundamentally different modes of behaviour for organizations and organisms. The former can restructure themselves internally (either as a result of conscious decisions or unconscious actions) in response to some environmental factor; and this change can occur rapidly. This is not true of organisms or biological systems; their structural adaptability to changing environments is slow and perhaps requires several generations.

Modern system theorists are moving away from a simple organic or deterministic stimulus-response model of change or behaviour. As Buckley says:

Modern 'cybernetic' systems theory

> . . . the behavior of complex open systems is not a simple and direct function of impinging external forces . . . Rather, as open systems become more complex there develop within them more and more complex mediating processes that intervene between external forces and behavior. At higher levels these mediating processes become more and more independent or autonomous, and more determinative of behavior . . . (Buckley 1967 p. 58.)

Buckley, and several other modern systems theorists, insist that we must move past the organic model to a cybernetic model, and deal with the flow of information (which includes ideas, attitudes, etc.). They try to make a fundamental connection with the 'action' perspective, suggesting that the perception of information relies on the meaning the receiver attaches to the information; its meaningfulness depends on him. The study of how people or groups in the system interpret its inputs and how these inputs create systems of meaning can lead to explanations of output behaviour. (Buckley 1973.)

As Chadwick puts it: 'Human systems are not like mechanical systems . . . each person, each group of persons, is a system which adapts and adjusts both to external and internal stimuli: . . . continually restructuring its perceived world in accordance with information flows received . . .' (Chadwick 1971 pp. 331–2.)

The paper by Buckley (1973) represents an attempt to make a bridge between systems theories of behaviour in organizations and the action approach. As we noted earlier, the emphasis moves away from the direct cause-effect model, in which inputs to the system directly determine behaviour, towards a model which include as mediatory process of perception and interpretation. In practice, this suggests that we

A bridge between system and action

must study the interaction between inputs of information and meanings, and attempt to understand the mechanism by which meanings and interpretations are generated.

2 Systems theory as a sociological tool

With its emphasis on managed equilibrium, systems theory, as applied to organization, has inevitably found some of its strongest support from managers and management consultants eager to solve problems of 'instability' and 'disequilibrium' in their organizations. Inevitably, therefore, there has been a tendency in systems analyses of organizations to accept as given the managers' notion of what constitutes a satisfactory equilibrium, and to accept the need to control and manage the behaviour of other members of the organization, so as to maintain this equilibrium or status quo. Thus systems analyses rarely contain any adequate examination of the nature of the power structure that confers on certain people in organizations the ability to make fundamental decisions affecting the structure and performance of the organization, and allows their goals to dominate the purposive behaviour of the organization. Systems models are fundamentally descriptions of *how* the system functions: they do not explain *why*. Why, for example, there arise fundamental conflicts of interest between sub-groups. For a satisfactory examination of such questions, we would have to return to more mainstream sociology.

In summary, it could be said that the systems perspective describes the structure and functioning of organizations and may reveal the nature and source of the factors determining the behaviour of the system. For example, we might be able to trace particular attitudes or actions of the members of the organization and relate these to economic inputs which impinge on the system from the environment. But, however well the systems approach describes the structure and explains certain behavioural phenomena, it does not explain why the structure, especially its power aspects, is as it is. To illuminate this would require a different approach to organizations.

Summary

3 Examples of applications of the systems approach to organizations

In previous sections we have introduced various systems approaches at a general theoretical level. In this final section you are referred to discussions in the set reading for this unit which deal with actual studies made on organizations using the systems approach. This should allow you to assess the status and effectiveness of systems models and systems approaches.

As we have mentioned, there are several systems approaches. Probably the best critical review of some of these approaches is in Silverman (1970): in the first five chapters he reviews the Parsonian equilibrium organic model, the socio-technical model of Emery, Trist *et al.* and a number of structural-functional systems approaches.

We have provided, as an offprint, a section from Eldridge's *Sociology and Industrial Life* (1971) entitled 'Systems Analysis and Industrial Behaviour'. This reviews the use of systems models in industrial sociology, including the human relations approach, the socio-technical approach and the open systems approach (Lupton and Goldthorpe are included in this latter category). Eldridge also discusses some of the more general systems approaches to organizations typical of the Tavistock Institutes research and the work of Jaques (1951) and Miller and Rice (1967). Much of this research, as you will see, has a prescriptive flavour.

Our second offprint is an attempt to give you some feel for the open socio-technical approach adopted by Emery and Trist in their study of coal mining and textile manufacture. The paper is entitled 'Socio-technical Systems' and deals with industrial organizations, mainly at the shop floor level.

Answer SAQ 1

The fact that organizations are made up of human individuals with differing attitudes and goals.

Answer SAQ 2

It may be the way the organization appears to operate, but it is not necessarily the leading goal of individuals in the organization. Also the organization may seek security through managing its environment, rather than maximizing its profit.

Answer SAQ 3

Once we realize that the central goal of the organization may not in fact be the operational goal for every sub-unit, we are in a position to reconsider the design of these sub-units. For example, in studies of work groups it has been found that groups exhibit a strong determination to run themselves and to be autonomous of external control. This goal is not necessarily in conflict with the managers' goal of high production – in fact it may be functional. The suggestion is that a systems view would identify these sub-goals and try to accommodate them in the overall structure.

Answer SAQ 4

Emery and Trist (see Offprint) suggest that work groups are not so much friendship based as task based: it does not appear that:

> ... the basic psychological needs being met by grouping are workers' needs for friendship on the job ... Grouping produces its main psychological effects when it leads to a system of work roles such that the workers are primarily related to each other by way of the requirements of task performance and task interdependence. (1969 pp. 31-2.)

Thus there is a complex interaction between group relations and technology: concentration on 'human relations' aspects independently from the technology would therefore be fruitless.

Answer SAQ 5

As you will have seen from Section 1.4 and from Figure 1, we have:

1 personnel
2 their attitudes and expectations
3 capital
4 technological knowledge
5 market forces (labour, capital and resource markets)
6 shareholders' demands.

Thus we have social and cultural 'inputs' as well as economic imperatives and technological changes.

References

ALBROW, M. (1973) 'The Study of Organizations – Objectivity or Bias?' in SALAMAN and THOMPSON (eds) pp. 396–413.

BENNIS, W. G. and THOMAS, J. M. (1972) *Management of Change and Conflict*, Harmondsworth, Penguin.

BUCKLEY, W. (1967) *Sociology and Modern Systems Theory*, Englewood Cliffs, Prentice Hall.

BUCKLEY, W. (1973) 'Society as a Complex Adaptive System' in SALAMAN and THOMPSON (eds) pp. 134–54.

BURNS, T. and STALKER, G. M. (1961) *The Management of Innovation*, London, Tavistock.

CHADWICK, G. (1971) *A Systems View of Planning*, Oxford, Pergamon Press.

CYERT, R. M. and MARCH, J. G. (1963) *A Behavioural Theory of the Firm*, Englewood Cliffs, Prentice Hall.

CHAMBERLAIN, N. W. (1948) *Union Challenge to Management Control*, New York, Harper and Brothers.

CHILD, J. (1973) 'Organizational Structure, Environment and Performance: The Role of Strategic Choice' in SALAMAN and THOMPSON (eds) pp. 91–107.

CLELAND, D. I. and KING, W. R. (1972) *Management: A Systems Approach*, New York, McGraw Hill.

COSER, L. A. (1956) *The Functions of Social Conflict*, London, Routledge and Kegan Paul.

DRUCKER, P. (1955) *The Practice of Management*, London, Heinemann.

ELDRIDGE, J. E. T. (1971) 'Systems Analysis and Industrial Behaviour' in ELDRIDGE, J. E. T., *Sociology and Industrial Life*, London, Michael Joseph, pp. 25–39.

EMERY, F. E. and TRIST, E. L. (1960) 'Socio-Technical Systems' in CHURCHMAN, C. W. and VERHULST, M. (eds) *Management Science, Models and Techniques*, Vol. 2, Oxford, Pergamon Press, pp. 83–97.

EMERY, F. E. and TRIST, E. L. (1969) 'The Causal Texture of Organizational Environment' in EMERY, F. (ed) *Systems Thinking*, Harmondsworth, Penguin, pp. 241–57.

ETZIONI, A. (1970) 'Two Approaches to Organizational Analysis: A Critique and a Suggestion' in GRUSKY and MILLER (eds) pp. 215–25.

GALBRAITH, J. K. (1967) *The New Industrial State*, London, Hamish Hamilton.

GOLDTHORPE, J. H., LOCKWOOD, D. *et al.* (1968) *The Affluent Worker: Industrial Attitudes and Behaviour*, Cambridge, Cambridge University Press.

GRUSKY, O. and MILLER, G. A. (eds) (1970) *The Sociology of Organizations: Basic Studies*, London, Collier-Macmillan (set book).

JAQUES, E. (1951) *The Changing Culture of a Factory*, London, Tavistock.

KATZ, D. and KAHN, R. L. (1970) 'Open-Systems Theory' in GRUSKY and MILLER (eds) pp. 149–58.

LAWRENCE, P. R. and LORSCH, J. W. (1967) *Organization and Environment*, Harvard, Harvard University.

LUPTON, T. and CUNNISON, S. (1964) 'Workshop Behaviour' in GLUCKMAN, M. (ed) *Closed Systems and Open Minds*, Edinburgh, Oliver and Boyd, pp. 103–28.

LUPTON, T. (1971) *Management and the Social Sciences*, Harmondsworth, Penguin.

MESAROVIC, M., SANDERS, J. L. and SPRAGUE, C. F. (1973) 'An Axiomatic Approach to Organizations From a General Systems Viewpoint' in OPTNER, L. (ed) *Systems Analysis*, Harmondsworth, Penguin, pp. 294–304.

MILLER, E. J. and RICE, A. K. (1967) *Systems of Organization*, London, Tavistock.

PARSONS, T. (1970) 'Social Systems' in GRUSKY and MILLER (eds) pp. 75–82.

PUGH, D. S., HICKSON, D. J. and HININGS, C. R. (1971) *Writers on Organizations*, Harmondsworth, Penguin.

ROETHLISBERGER, F. J. and DICKSON, W. J. (1970) 'Human Relations' in GRUSKY and MILLER (eds) pp. 53–63.

SALAMAN, G. and THOMPSON, K. (eds) (1973) *People and Organizations*, London, Longmans (the Reader).

SILVERMAN, D. (1970) *The Theory of Organizations*, London, Heinemann (set book).

SIMON, H. (1945) *Administrative Behaviour*, London, Macmillan.

SIMON, H. (1969) 'On the Concept of Organizational Goal' in ETZIONI, A. (ed) *A Sociological Reader on Complex Organizations*, London, Holt Rinehart and Winston, pp. 158–74.

SPENCER, H. (1897) *Principles of Sociology*, London, Appleton-Century Crofts. Third edition.

WOODWARD, J. (1959) *Management and Technology*, London, HMSO.

Acknowledgement

Ruth Elliott assisted in writing the final draft of this unit.